Education and the World View

The Council on Learning established its Education and the World View program in an effort to encourage the nation's colleges and universities to widen the international components in their undergraduate curriculum. The Council sponsors this public program because a more consonant reflection of current world realities in education lies in the best interests of the nation as well as its citizens. This program has been funded by the National Endowment for the Humanities, the United States Department of Education, the Exxon Education Foundation, and the Joyce Mertz-Gilmore Foundation. The various activities under this endeavor are guided by a national task force of 50 leaders in academic, public, and business life. For further information about this project, write to the Council on Learning, 271 North Avenue, New Rochelle, N.Y. 10801.

March 1981; second printing January 1982

This handbook on exemplary international undergraduate programs is one of a series of Council on Learning publications on global perspectives in American higher education. Others in this series, listed at the end of this volume, may also be ordered from Change Magazine Press. This book and the Education and the World View Project have received support from the National Endowment for the Humanities and the Exxon Education Foundation.

Council on Learning

Education for a Global Century:
Handbook of
Exemplary International Programs

Change Magazine Press

1981

Contents

Consortia   133

More Good Ideas   147

Thematic Index   155

INTRODUCTION

Throughout the work of the Education and the World View (E&WV) project, it was a major tenet of the Council on Learning that much of the further development of international dimensions in American undergraduate learning must come of necessity out of the efforts of the colleges and universities themselves. This approach admittedly goes against much of the grain of international education programs which traditionally have relied heavily on external foundation and federal support.

It is now likely that, from here on out, local and regional initiatives will continue to grow in their creative importance. What the E&WV project finds is that many effective international programs and approaches have already become significant, some conducted with purely institutional resources, others with a minimum of seed money that permitted accelerated implementation. Despite higher education's best lobbying efforts, federal outlays for international education are not likely to grow in dramatic ways, particularly not at the undergraduate level. Campus initiatives can thrive, however, through the development of networks and proven talents. As institutions learn from each other, adaptive and effective programs that best fit the character of each are thus developed and enter the curriculum.

It is important to recognize what this handbook of exemplary programs is and what it is not. There was no intent to select the "top" 50-odd programs or approaches in the United States. Such obviously subjective judgments would serve no useful purpose. The selections in this volume met certain criteria, the most important of which remain ease of adaptability and effectiveness in reaching growing numbers of students, while not placing an exorbitant strain on institutional budgets.

After a full evaluation by the Council's project staff and task force members, descriptions of selected campus programs were provided by the institutions themselves and edited by the Council on Learning. As these exemplars were culled from an original evaluation list of some 200, not all described in this volume could be visited and those finally selected received close scrutiny by other means. We believe these descriptions to be essentially correct and worth citing in this national roster.

The obligation of the listed academic institutions is the willingness to share their experiences with colleagues elsewhere. Readers of this handbook are encouraged to make reasonable use of the contacts provided. Because of the increase in effective uses of interinstitutional cooperation, we have also provided a short section on selected consortia; and, since we encountered far too many good ideas that should not be overlooked, there are also brief descriptions of additional interesting ideas from around the country.

The survey of programs was conducted by the E&WV project director, Robert Black, as well as by our programs associate, Grace Hechinger, and Peter Warren White, a research associate at Columbia University. This handbook, along with related publications, provides a highly useful set of practical tools for the development of college offerings that befit a new world of extraordinary complexity urgently requiring better comprehension by the nation's college students.

George W. Bonham
Chairman
E&WV National Advisory Board

Selecting the Listings

The programs and approaches featured in this book were selected in a three-phase process. The preliminary task was to determine the best criteria for identifying and evaluating programs and institutions. The second was to survey the catalogs of the nation's 3,200 two- and four-year colleges and universities. Numerous national and regional educational organizations, authorities in language and international studies, and nonacademic institutions in international and intercultural affairs were consulted throughout these phases. Their cooperation is gratefully acknowledged.

About 200 colleges and universities and a number of curriculum-related consortia were identified as having the rudiments of excellent programs. After initial staff evaluation, a pretested survey questionnaire was sent to approximately 160 campuses. The questionnaire covered curricular strategies, faculty involvement, student life and extracurricular environments, learning resources, enrollments and majors, and other points. Some 20 campuses and 10 consortia were visited during the identification and evaluation process. The basic campus information was provided by the institutions selected. Consortia descriptions and the section on other ideas were prepared by the Council from requested materials.

The overall findings show some significant common features in effective programs, regardless of discipline, institution size, resource base, and so on:

- a genuine commitment by top faculty and administrators to have significant international dimensions in the curriculum;

- pedagogical merit and soundness of what is taught, offered, or proposed;

- faculty involvement from the start, especially if initiatives have come from the administration;

- consideration for the needs and interests of student constituencies;

- prior review of other institutions and programs to see what may be innovative or usable or adaptable to campus needs and capabilities;

- consortial approaches to make effective use of scarce resources or expand in new directions;

- an early introduction of students into other countries and cultures so they benefit exponentially from what they experience;

- multidisciplinary if not interdisciplinary approaches, to reflect a world that is not divided into departments but into issues;

- working with what is already in place rather than trying to create new programs out of whole cloth;

- critical leadership by those on campus who take initiative in diplomatic but energetic ways.

The caveat in these findings and in the national listings is that these are not the only strong, effective undergraduate programs and approaches. But they are representative and feasible examples upon whose experiences others may profitably draw.

Robert Black
E&WV Project Director

I

Exemplary Programs

The campus descriptions following are arranged alphabetically. Each includes a brief introduction of the institution, an overview of the international aspects of the curriculum, how these are organized, and their educational impact. Resource persons listed may be contacted for further information. Also refer to categorical listings on page 155.

BREVARD COMMUNITY COLLEGE, Cocoa, FL

Established in 1960, Brevard is a two-year, coeducational, publicly supported community college. Its campuses and centers serve more than 9,800 full-time students and a total of 33,000 Brevard County residents annually. There are 34 preprofessional university parallel programs, 34 occupational and technical programs, and 26 certificate programs. A majority have an international perspective, accomplished through course revisions made by faculty. Cross-cultural workshops and seminars are conducted regularly for faculty to broaden their global understanding and to upgrade teaching methods.

INTERNATIONAL ASPECTS OF THE CURRICULUM. Brevard offers an AA in international/intercultural studies. This is a university-parallel major coordinated with universities; the student may transfer with junior standing to an upper-level institution. The International Studies Program is built around a cross-cultural approach to general education requirements, with an emphasis on area studies and languages.

The International Studies Program, the Foreign Language Program, and the International Student Program are organized into one collegewide division and use many of the same resources. For example, foreign students assist as native speakers in language courses (Spanish, German, French, Portuguese, Arabic, etc.) and also help in international studies and area studies courses.

Virtually all departments are involved with the International Studies Division, which is funded by the college ($75,000) and by federal grants ($50,000).

HOW ORGANIZED. Almost the entire curriculum of Brevard has international dimensions. New courses include Introduction to International/Intercultural Studies, Introduction to Latin-American Studies, Introduction to the Middle East, Geography of World Societies, Arabic Language, Second Language Internship, and Human Adjustment. Mutual learning between international and American students is emphasized. For example, some American majors in languages and international studies are enrolled in an orientation/adjustment course called Human Adjustment Psychology, required of all new international students.

Programs and courses are continually evaluated by students, faculty, administrators, and outside consultants. All aspects of this international emphasis have become a permanent part of the curriculum.

EDUCATIONAL IMPACT. The international dimension at Brevard has affected every area and department. Administration and faculty support the program. Under U.S. Department of Education funding, and because of general interest, all courses and programs have global emphasis. Faculty from disparate areas have worked together in seminars and workshops to develop international courses and syllabi. Strong student response reflects this approach. Approximately 400 are directly involved in international programs.

Brevard is the coordinating institution of the Community College Cooperative for International Development (CCCID). This consortium arranges at the uppermost levels faculty and resource exchanges among its members and a number of countries, as well as some special student exchanges. The effect of Brevard's

CCCID activity is seen mostly in faculty renewal and development, resulting in widened international dimensions in courses.

RESOURCE PERSON. Edward D. Fitchen, Dean of International Studies, Brevard Community College, 1519 Clearlake Road, Cocoa, FL 32922. Phone: (305) 632-1111, x254/309.

THE CALIFORNIA STATE UNIVERSITY AND COLLEGES,
Long Beach, CA

The California State University and Colleges (CSUC) includes 19 campuses brought together as a system in 1960, although the oldest campus was founded in 1857. CSUC is supported by public funds and is essentially free to qualified residents of California. CSUC offers more than 1,400 bachelor's and master's programs in over 200 subject areas. A limited number of doctorates are offered jointly with other institutions. Enrollments in 1979 totaled over 300,000, of whom 96 percent were California residents. Full-time faculty numbered 15,000. Last year CSUC awarded over 52 percent of the bachelor's degrees and 32 percent of the master's degrees in California.

INTERNATIONAL ASPECTS OF THE CURRICULUM. Since 1963 CSUC has maintained an official study-abroad unit, the *Office of International Programs*, in which students enroll simultaneously at one of the CSUC campuses and in a foreign university or special study program abroad for a full academic year. Participants remain regularly registered students, technically in residence at their home campuses. All overseas course work is accepted by the students' campuses as residence credit, although courses are not necessarily applied to meet requirements in the major.

Specialized centers are maintained in Denmark (architecture, international business), Italy (architecture, art history), New Zealand (agriculture), and Sweden (limnology). More general curricular offerings are available in Brazil, France, Germany, Israel, Japan, Mexico, Peru, Quebec, the Republic of China, and Spain. Selection is competitive and limited to upper-division undergraduates and graduate students. At least two years of college-level language study is required for the Brazil, France, Germany, Mexico, Peru, Quebec, and Spain programs. Approximately 400 are enrolled in the international programs each year.

HOW ORGANIZED. Overseas study centers have a resident director, usually a CSUC faculty member, responsible for the academic, administrative, and advising aspects of the program abroad. In many centers the program begins with a Preparatory Language Program that aids in language acquisition and cultural adaptation. Thereafter course work depends principally on the individual student's language proficiency and academic background. Three basic types of courses are offered, which vary by country and by program: those sponsored directly by the program for CSUC students only, those sponsored by the host university for foreign students in general, and others sponsored by the host university for all students as a regular part of the curriculum. Fluent, qualified students are encouraged to take the regular university courses.

Students pay for predeparture processing, travel, insurance, housing and meals, and home campus registration fees. International programs are supported by state funds to the extent that such funds would have been expended had the student continued to study at the home campus. The state thus supports all instructional and administrative costs associated with program operation.

EDUCATIONAL IMPACT. Since 1963 international programs have permitted some 6,000 CSUC students to study full time for an academic year in a foreign country, affiliated with a foreign university. Students have gained firsthand knowledge and understanding of other areas of the world while making normal progress toward their degrees. In most cases the skills and knowledge acquired have been demonstrably advantageous in preparing these students for careers in teaching, government service, and world trade. Language instruction on campus has been encouraged since there is practical opportunity to use a foreign tongue. More important, international programs have enhanced international dimensions on each campus by offering to students the curricular option of living and functioning in other cultures and value systems.

RESOURCE PERSON. Kibbey M. Horne, Director of International Programs, Office of the Chancellor, CSUC, 400 Golden Shore, Long Beach, CA 90802. Phone: (213) 590-5655.

CENTRAL COLLEGE OF IOWA, Pella, IA

Founded in 1853, Central is a private, four-year, coeducational liberal arts college. More than 1,500 students are enrolled on the home campus and on 6 international campuses (Paris, Vienna, Granada, London, Carmarthen, Merida, Yucatan). Majors are offered in 35 areas by 73 full-time and 27 part-time faculty. Over 60 percent of full-time faculty hold doctorates. The Division of Cross-Cultural Studies is located in the recently remodeled International Studies Center.

INTERNATIONAL ASPECTS OF THE CURRICULUM. Departments at Central College are assembled into six divisions. The Division of Cross-Cultural Studies includes the departments of French, German, and Spanish; it also provides instruction in Dutch, Greek, Hebrew, and Portuguese. Nearly 10 percent of course credits taken at Central are from this division. The number of students who major in a language is about five times greater than the national average.

Nearly half of Central's students study at one or more of the college's international centers. Nearly all who major in French, German, or Spanish spend a full year studying the language abroad; there is also a semester option.

Central provides language houses for students with adequate French, German, and Spanish. Those returning from study abroad and native speakers from the home country live here with students preparing to go abroad. Every effort is made to ensure that residents use the country's language for all conversations.

For those who choose not to study a language intensively or participate in one of Central's English-speaking international programs, the cross-cultural studies division provides two options. A course entitled Cross-Cultural Communications and Perceptions seeks to present a philosophical, valuational rationale for international studies; establish a theoretical framework for study in cross-cultural perception and communication; and develop practical techniques for facilitating cross-cultural adjustment. The second option, three courses entitled Introduction to French/German/Spanish Culture and Language, provides beginning language skills and structure, combined with readings and discussion (in English).

HOW ORGANIZED. Central's entire international studies program is supervised by the dean of the college. With advice from the faculty Council on International Programs, which includes the chairs of the French, German, and Spanish departments as ex officio voting members, the dean oversees the programs abroad and the cross-cultural emphasis on the home campus.

Individual language departments within cross-cultural studies take the lead in emphasizing the importance of study abroad for each major. It is required for the major, in the belief that this contributes substantially to fluency.

The French and Spanish department chairmen have received training from the U.S. Department of State Foreign Service Institute in the FSI method of oral competency testing, now used on campus in these languages. The German department is planning to develop similar testing methods.

Each study center abroad is required to generate the necessary tuition income to pay its share of total expenses. Costs (exclusive of boarding) for the full 1981-82 academic year vary from a low of $4,800 in Paris (10 months) to a high of $5,950 in Vienna (11 months).

EDUCATIONAL IMPACT. Central College began international education in the late 1940s with exploratory programming in Mexico. During the 1960s the experiment became a permanent and integral part of the program. International education has become a trademark for Central College. Students from about 500 colleges have participated as a result of Central's system of cooperating colleges and national recruitment for study at its European centers.

At home the International Studies Center flies the flag of each nation hosting one of Central's campuses. The center is now a well-established feature. Emphasis on global understanding pervades the campus and the curriculum; study-abroad programs have become a matter of pride for the campus.

RESOURCE PERSON. Harold M. Kolenbrander, Central College, Pella, IA 50219. Phone: (515) 628-4151, x271.

CENTRAL VIRGINIA COMMUNITY COLLEGE, Lynchburg, VA

Central Virginia Community College, established in 1967, is part of the Virginia Community College System. CVCC serves about 190,000 in the cities of Lynchburg and Bedford and four surrounding counties. The college offers comprehensive programs to prepare students for four-year colleges. Recent enrollment was 1,140 full-time and 2,830 part-time students in 38 programs, a 16 percent increase over the previous year. Surveys conducted during 1979-80 indicate that roughly two thirds of college transfer graduates and former students entered four-year colleges or universities, while about 85 percent of occupational/technical graduates and former students are employed. The faculty of 75 full-time instructors and 81 part-time lecturers is organized into six divisions. The college has an annual budget of $3.9 million.

INTERNATIONAL ASPECTS OF THE CURRICULUM. Area studies at Central Virginia Community College are primarily related to the study of foreign languages, under the auspices of the recently established *Cross-Cultural and Foreign Language Resource Center*. The center is an activity rather than a physical entity and aims for maximum use of facilities of the Division of Learning Resources: two language labs, a learning laboratory, and a TV studio.

The foreign language and cross-cultural program was developed primarily to help the public and college communities become more familiar with other languages and diverse cultures. While demand for languages from the traditional liberal arts student is not increasing significantly, the need for special or short-term instruction in a variety of languages is growing. Local businesses and industries need language instruction for their representatives to foreign clients, as demonstrated by on-site programs created for employees. Moreover, the international business interests of many area corporations promise a continuing and increasing demand for language and cross-cultural education.

English as a second language is needed by the growing community of Indochinese refugees, Middle Eastern students, and other groups (such as employees and families associated with German-American companies in the central Virginia area). The functions of the center include an outreach program aimed at minorities, senior citizens, and others who, lacking funds or appropriate guidance, fail to take advantage of multicultural enrichment education.

HOW ORGANIZED. CVCC's foreign language and cross-cultural program was made possible through a consultancy grant (1977) and a pilot grant (1979) awarded by the National Endowment for the Humanities. The cross-cultural center coordinator, an assistant professor of foreign languages from the Division of Humanities, directs the program and also serves as NEH project director. He is assisted by a history professor from the Division of Social Sciences and by an instructional assistant and an audiovisual technician from the Division of Learning Resources.

Although the program focuses on individualized, self-paced language instruction and a broader understanding of culture through language skills, it also uses minicourses, workshops, seminars, and short presentations to meet the needs of specific groups. The use of cable TV is planned. Most of these activities are offered in cooperation with the Division of Continuing Education.

The self-paced program includes introductory courses in Arabic, Chinese, French, German, Japanese, Portuguese, and Spanish—languages of importance for trade and sociopolitical communication. "Cultural Packages" complement and support the language instruction. The cultural data include brief historical background, cultural institutions (education), political and legal structures, art, music, customs, and food. For minicourses, workshops, and seminars, instruction and presentations are given through interdisciplinary cooperation.

EDUCATIONAL IMPACT. The foreign language and cross-cultural program has been very favorably received throughout the college and the community. A key element in the program's development has been the assistance of the three senior colleges in the central Virginia area. Faculty from Lynchburg College, Randolph-Macon Woman's College, and Sweet Briar College, acting as consultants, worked closely with the project director on the cultural booklets for the European, Middle Eastern, and Asian countries selected for the study.

The program's growing popularity is confirmed by the number of community residents using the audiovisual materials; high school teachers visiting to become familiar with the new instructional devices; increasing requests for information from institutions and individuals, within the state and elsewhere; and invitations to the coordinator to participate as consultant and presenter in local, regional, and national conferences and workshops such as the Foreign Language Teachers Workshop at Virginia Polytechnic Institute and State University, the NEH Workshop in Puerto Rico, and the AAJC Workshop in Baltimore.

Additionally, demand is increasing for language courses at plants. Danish and Spanish have been taught at GE. The one-year Danish Language and Culture course enrolled 30 students; 27 took the two-year Spanish Language and Culture course; and a summer Spanish Conversation and Culture course enrolled 22, mostly engineers, technicians, and administrators. Employees of Meredith/Burda Inc., a German-American company, have been attending evening classes in German on campus.

RESOURCE PERSON. Eduardo A. Peniche, Assistant Professor of Foreign Languages, Division of Humanities, Central Virginia Community College, PO Box 4098, Lynchburg, VA 24502. Phone: (804) 239-0321, x353/218.

COLGATE UNIVERSITY, Hamilton, NY

Colgate was founded in 1817, originally to train and educate young men for the ministry. It became Madison University in 1846 by charter from the state legislature. The name was changed to Colgate in 1890 to recognize the Colgate family's generosity. It is now primarily a coed 4-year liberal arts college with 2,600 undergraduates and 160 full-time faculty; 85 percent have doctoral degrees. The college's annual budget is $24 million and it has an endowment of $40 million. Colgate offers 37 concentrations, including several interdisciplinary choices, and 18 off-campus study groups. It also has a small graduate program offering MA and MAT degrees in several fields. A January intersession is part of its year-round program. Approximately 86 percent of all freshmen graduate.

INTERNATIONAL ASPECTS OF THE CURRICULUM. Colgate has four international programs that operate independently to serve different student interests. Most career directed is the international relations (IR) concentration, based on designated courses in economics, history, and political science, or foreign languages. Many of these students enter government, business, or education; in 1980 there were some 90 concentrators.

Peace and World Order Studies (PEST) is an interdisciplinary program begun in 1970 that deals with armed conflict, social justice, economic well-being, and ecological balance. It emphasizes problem solving through alternative world structures, political means, and study of the future. The concentration requires ten courses: two interdisciplinary peace studies courses, others on international ethics and international affairs, two seminars, and an off-campus internship with some organization working for peace or on other world order problems. PEST students are encouraged to live in Ralph Bunche House, the center for public affairs activities, under the graduate resident advisor, who is also the peace intern. Program graduates enter law, service organizations, and education. In 1980 there were 15 concentrators.

The general education segment requires every Colgate junior or senior to select one course about a culture other than his or her own. Most study a single "emerging society," taught by a faculty specialist usually in the social sciences; there are other options, such as taking three related departmental courses or joining an overseas study group (except to Great Britain). In each semester about 600 students are enrolled.

Some overseas study groups focus on one discipline; others are more varied. But all must include a systematic study of the host culture. Lectures or full courses are given by faculty and officials of the host country. Students prepare research papers or detailed journals for Colgate credit. Seventeen foreign areas have received the groups; in any year fifteen to sixteen groups (about two hundred students) go abroad. Similar trips are occasionally made during the January intersession.

HOW ORGANIZED. Colgate has no overall guiding body for its international instruction. The IR program is led by political science faculty, who also serve as academic advisors. Peace and World Order Studies is under a faculty director whose main tasks are to get more staff from different departments to join PEST's interdisciplinary courses; to add appropriate courses from relevant fields; and to persuade departments to release members for half time in PEST. The faculty director of the emerging societies requirement (or its equivalent) has a similar staffing problem, though there is far less supervision of course content. Overseas study groups are arranged by each instructor or department concerned, subject to university approval for costs, academic quality, and availability of courses in the instructor's absence.

Budgets vary widely. There is no special funding for IR and the general education program. PEST draws on a generous grant made some years ago by an alumnus, and now covers the peace intern-Bunche House resident advisor at $5,500, as well as costs of staff travel and campus speakers and films. Overseas study groups are supported by participants' tuitions; usually, 15 to 20 students comprise a group. More costly trips may be financed by outside sources.

EDUCATIONAL IMPACT.   Most programs are old enough so that curriculum support is well established, especially in languages. More gratifying, however, are the activities that reveal their impact through student-arranged lectures and panels by faculty and visitors, plus films and social events. The IR Club stays mostly with international relations issues, while Bunche House is the center for weekly programs on any of the four PEST concerns. Students participate in off-campus activities related to international and global topics and speak in nearby communities. A most productive experience has been PEST concentrators' reports on their internships with social change organizations in the United States and abroad. The careers peace interns enter often set a mark for undergraduate concern for social change.

RESOURCE PERSON.   Andrew Rembert, Assistant Dean of Faculty, Colgate University, Hamilton, NY 13346. Phone: (315) 824-1000, x216.

DICKINSON COLLEGE, Carlisle, PA

Dickinson is an independent liberal arts college committed to undergraduate general education and professional preparation. Founded in 1773 by Presbyterians, it graduated its first class in 1787 and since 1833 has been related to the Methodist Church. The college has been coeducational since 1886; currently men and women are enrolled in about equal numbers. There are 1,650 matriculated students on campus and 150 in off-campus study programs. Most students are from the eastern seaboard. Dickinson awards the BA and BS. There are 115 full-time faculty, 90 percent of whom hold a PhD or equivalent, and an additional 25 academic professionals. The library has 300,000 volumes. Dickinson's 1980-81 budget is $15 million; its endowment is $19 million. Of entering freshmen, 75 percent graduate within four years, and half of those continue their studies.

INTERNATIONAL ASPECTS OF THE CURRICULUM. Dickinson takes a three-tiered approach to international education. Language instruction, area studies majors, and off-campus studies are part of a complex of opportunities.

Language through the intermediate level is required of all Dickinson graduates, about a quarter of whom work beyond that point. Majors are offered in French, German, Spanish, Latin, and Greek and oral communication skills are emphasized equally with the capacity to read a culture's literature. Advanced work is available in literature and in civilization topics. Minors are offered in additional languages—Italian, Russian, and ancient Hebrew. Through guided independent study and validation by outside examiners, work through the intermediate level is available in Portuguese, Japanese, and Chinese.

Though Dickinson is organized departmentally by traditional liberal arts disciplines, it offers interdisciplinary majors, minors, and certification programs in area studies. The International Studies major graduates about 20 students a year who have complemented a breadth of methodology and theory courses with depth in a geographic area—Latin America, Europe, the Middle East, or China-Japan. The Russian and Soviet Area Studies major graduates about five students, and approximately ten complete a certification program (augmented minor) in Latin-American Studies. The latter two programs require language proficiency; though a language is not a must for students majoring in International Studies, most have a second major in a modern language.

About one fourth of juniors study overseas, half of those for a full academic year. Dickinson runs its own Center for European Studies in Bologna, Italy (30 students a year) and a Colombia Semester program in Medellin (10 students). Another 100 study at European universities or elsewhere in a variety of cooperative programs and through individual arrangements they make with the assistance of the director of off-campus studies. Internships overseas are encouraged.

All students must take one Comparative Civilizations course in which non-Western materials are studied from a perspective that encourages comparative analysis and appreciation. Weekly language tables, an International House dorm, participation in such events as Model UNs, and a language-based summer study program in France reinforce the primary three tiers.

HOW ORGANIZED. All elements of the international study opportunities at Dickinson are supported by the regular college budget. The language programs are run by the appropriate departments (French and Italian, Spanish, German and Russian). Area studies are coordinated by committees of faculty drawn from the humanities and social sciences. Special seminars required of senior majors in an area studies field are contributed by the participating departments, as are courses satisfying the Comparative Civilizations graduation requirement. The center at Bologna is staffed full time by a Dickinson faculty member. Because of this integrated approach it is difficult to determine precisely what proportion of the budget directly supports global studies.

Students choose courses in these disciplines and areas through the registration processes used for all course enrollment. They are guided by faculty advising and by the Off-Campus Studies and Internship offices and are encouraged to see how language facility, area studies, and firsthand experience within a foreign culture can be integrated. Since many participating students are double majors, the international dimension may be added via a complex of pathways.

A Committee on International Education coordinates these arrangements. It is composed of representatives from each area study program, each of the modern languages, and Comparative Civilizations, as well as the dean of the college and one of the assistant deans. Committee oversight is provided by the Academic Program Committee and its Off-Campus Studies subcommittee.

EDUCATIONAL IMPACT. The humanities and social sciences faculty are involved in interlacing ways in the support of Dickinson's international study offerings. These involvements are recognized as appropriate arenas for teaching and research, and therefore are seen by the departments as an aspect of their primary mission. Faculty are exploring ways to increase this participation, and to include the arts and the natural sciences (through history of science). Three faculty now have formal interdisciplinary appointments, of which one portion is in an area studies program.

Students perceive Dickinson as providing strong internationalist programs; even many who have no intention of participating say they decided to come to the college in part because of this dimension to its curriculum. The international offerings balance the college's emphasis on American studies and its concern with national heritage befitting the United States' colonial origins.

RESOURCE PERSON. George Allan, Dean, Dickinson College, Carlisle, PA 17013. Phone: (717) 245-1321.

DONNELLY COLLEGE, Kansas City, KS

A two-year, independent, coeducational community college, Donnelly was founded in 1949 and is affiliated with the Catholic Church. It is sponsored by the Archdiocese of Kansas City, Kansas, and has a four-acre campus in Kansas City. Over 760 students are enrolled; women comprise 52 percent of the student body and the average age is 27. The faculty number 17 full-time and 32 part-time instructors. Donnelly serves a very diverse student population—there are 55 percent blacks, 21 percent whites, 22 percent international students, and 2 percent Asians in the degree programs. Students come from 25 countries. In cooperation with St. Mary College, Leavenworth, KS, graduates may complete their higher education in the "2 Plus Two" Program on the Donnelly campus in accounting, business administration, and public affairs. Donnelly pretechnology students may also transfer into the higher degree programs at Pittsburg State University. Approximately 65 percent of Donnelly graduates continue their education. Donnelly College's annual budget is $1,600,915.

INTERNATIONAL ASPECTS OF THE CURRICULUM. The objectives of Donnelly's *World Studies Program* concern the total educational process in instruction and supporting activities. Two AA degrees, in international relations and in world studies-economics, were prepared over a two-year period, financed by a grant from the U.S. Department of Education. Before and during this curriculum development, several workshops and consultations were conducted in order to give the entire college community the rationale for a world view. The critical languages offerings are 15 languages that students may take by arrangement with qualified instructors. The World Studies Program covers the entire curriculum, and each department rewrote goals and objectives to include the international dimension. As a result, every student at Donnelly benefits from the program. Although most international courses for the AA are in humanities and social sciences, new courses in other departments have also been designed. Cultural anthropology and world geography are two of the newest.

Another objective of the World Studies Program is to sensitize not only the campus but the local community as well—through cultural presentations, speakers on international affairs, and dialogue with foreign students on campus (usually about 200). The college holds an annual International Fair Day, with booths (sponsored by students and faculty) displaying different cultures. International speakers and performers are engaged by Donnelly throughout the year. These activities supplement the cultural impact of the International Fair Day.

HOW ORGANIZED. One goal at Donnelly is to incorporate and emphasize the global aspect of education in all phases of learning. The director of the World Studies Program interviews students and presents the world studies courses leading to the AA degrees. Two local four-year colleges, St. Mary and the University of Kansas at Lawrence, offer degrees in international studies. Planning and cooperation with directors of the four-year programs ensure a smooth transition. The World Studies Program is evaluated in terms of the needs of the prospective degree candidate. Questionnaires are also distributed to a cross-section of all Donnelly students to ascertain the effect of the program on the whole college population.

The Steering Committee of the program provides an opportunity for members to share views with students by holding panel discussions, at which students make presentations on international aspects of their classroom experiences. Many referrals for World Studies Program candidates come from instructors who are also student advisors. The local media have helped publicize Donnelly's international education endeavors.

EDUCATIONAL IMPACT. Donnelly held three workshops to make administration, faculty, and staff aware of the One World Program. One was on the international education concept and the other two were on Peace and Justice, the Catholic Church's program that relates to global perspectives in education. These workshops solidified acceptance of the international program already in place at Donnelly. An ongoing effort by the Steering Committee assured the local, civic, and diocesan community that Donnelly was sincere in its effort to further international education. One indicator of the World Studies Program's success is the increase in enrollees; 526 students took the world studies courses offered during 1979-80. Also, the critical languages segment doubled its enrollment.

RESOURCE PERSON. Sr. Martha Ann Linck, Donnelly College, 1236 Sandusky Avenue, Kansas City, KS 66102. Phone: (913) 621-6070, x36.

DREW UNIVERSITY, Madison, NJ

Drew University, founded in 1866, is a fully accredited independent institution of-fering coeducational programs in the liberal arts and graduate and theological education. Its historic affiliation is with the United Methodist Church. The College of Liberal Arts offers the BA in 26 fields and enrolls 1,500 students, 70 percent of whom go on for postgraduate study. The Graduate School, with an enrollment of 300, offers MA and PhD degrees in English literature, nineteenth-century studies, and a variety of religious and theological programs. The Theological School enrolls 485 students and offers 6 degrees. Full-time faculty totals 111. Drew's endowment is valued at approximately $28 million. The campus is located on 186 acres in Madison, N.J. Rose Memorial Library houses nearly 500,000 volumes. In 1980 the Gamma Chapter of Phi Beta Kappa was installed.

INTERNATIONAL ASPECTS OF THE CURRICULUM. Drew University has a broad and very deep commitment to international studies. Three semester-long programs are conducted in London, Brussels, and at the United Nations in New York City. Approximately 220 students participate annually, earning up to 15 credit hours. About half are regular Drew students; the rest come from universities and colleges across the United States.

The *London Semester*, given in both fall and spring, offers courses in comparative political science, economics, and history, with heavy emphasis on the British political system. Students are taught by British faculty from Oxford, Cambridge, the London School of Economics, and Essex, and by a British member of parliament and a full-time Drew faculty member. There are numerous government speakers and a major on-site research project. Students live in a London hotel leased by the university and classes are conducted at the Royal Commonwealth Society.

The *Semester on the United Nations*, given in both fall and spring, provides an insight into international diplomacy. Approximately 30 guest speakers from the Secretariat and the diplomatic corps meet with participants and two Drew faculty twice a week in the university's facilities directly across from the UN headquarters. Subjects include UN organization and processes, peacekeeping, problems of development, and global management. Students live on the Drew campus during their stay and commute to New York twice a week on a chartered bus. Nine credit hours are earned in the program, with the remaining hours taken from the regular Drew offerings.

The *Semester on the European Community* (EC) focuses on the European integration process from the historical, political, and economic perspectives. Classes are taught by European faculty drawn from the College of Europe and from the Universities of Brussels and Louvain; there is a colloquium series dealing with current issues, and students prepare a major research project. Actual research at the headquarters of the European Communities in Brussels is stressed. Classes are held at the Institute of European Studies at the University of Brussels, and students live in private homes in the vicinity. Trips are scheduled to Luxembourg and Strasbourg to view other EC organizations at work. Travel grants from the Francqui Foundation help defer transportation costs. Knowledge of a European language is helpful.

HOW ORGANIZED. Drew's international programs have three common objectives. First, they expose students to a wide variety of practitioners within the United Nations, the European Communities, and the British government. There is a heavy emphasis on guest speakers and instructors, and students are encouraged to interview key personnel. Second, on-site field research is an integral part of each student's experience. All three programs require a major research project. Third, each of the programs must be of the highest academic caliber.

The three international semesters are directly controlled by two departments in the College of Liberal Arts. The Semester on the United Nations and the London Semester are run by the Department of Political Science, while the Semester on the European Community is headed by the Department of Economics. Full-time faculty are designated resident directors of each program and they have on-site supervisory and teaching responsibilities. There is a coordinator of off-campus programs who works directly for the associate dean of the College of Liberal Arts. The coordinator processes applications, sends out recruitment materials, answers inquiries, helps students prepare for overseas, and keeps records.

With the exception of a modest travel grant from the Francqui Foundation for the program in Brussels, all three semesters are financially self-sufficient, with operating expenses fully met by tuition charges. Annual budgets for each program total approximately $185,000 for London, $87,000 for Brussels, and $58,000 for the United Nations Program. Students pay travel expenses to and from Brussels and London. Limited financial aid is available.

EDUCATIONAL IMPACT.   Since the 1960s the United Nations, London, and European Community programs have had a profound impact on global awareness throughout the university community. In addition, approximately 2,600 students from nearly 300 universities and colleges across the United States have participated. There is little doubt that these students return to their campuses with an enhanced appreciation of global concerns. There is widespread faculty support for these programs at Drew and all three currently operate at or near capacity, attesting to their popularity among students. They are widely recognized and appreciated within the United Nations as well as in the European Communities and in the British government.

As the benefits of overseas study have been made obvious, other departments have added overseas courses during the January term or in conjunction with summer school. These include such courses as mythology taught in Athens, history taught in Moscow, botany taught in Puerto Rico, archaeology in the Middle East, English literature taught in London, and language programs in Paris and Madrid. These programs enhance the international awareness and outreach of both faculty and students.

RESOURCE PERSON.   Vivian Bull, Associate Dean, College of Liberal Arts, BC-106, Drew University, Madison, NJ 07940. Phone: (201) 377-3000, x325.

EASTERN KENTUCKY UNIVERSITY, Richmond, KY

Eastern Kentucky University (EKU) is a regional coeducational public institution that offers general and liberal arts programs and preprofessional and professional training in education and other fields at the undergraduate and graduate levels. It was founded in 1874 as a teachers' college called Central University and was renamed in 1966. Over 14,000 are enrolled. EKU has 602 full-time and 121 part-time faculty, of which 53 percent have doctorates. The institution's annual budget is $49.2 million.

INTERNATIONAL ASPECTS OF THE CURRICULUM. EKU offers a wide variety of international or global studies courses taught in traditional departments—history, geography, political science, and languages. In addition, three interdisciplinary departments—social science, humanities, and natural science—were created in the 1960s exclusively to teach undergraduate general education courses, all designed to help students develop a global perspective.

The Department of Social Science offers a program designed to help students link the past and present and anticipate trends and developments. This is accomplished by a sequence of four courses that analyze the story of mankind from prehistory to the present. The program is built around mankind's progression from a hunting to an agrarian to an industrial life. The Agrarian and Industrial revolutions are the linchpins.

Selected cultural heritages—such as the Chinese, Indian, Middle Eastern, African, and western European—are analyzed: how they developed in relative isolation in the preindustrial period and how they are adjusting to industrialism in today's interdependent world. Contemporary issues such as population, pollution, energy, and uneven economic development are examined in a global context.

The Department of Humanities has a sequence of four courses that examine aspects of the human experience. An interdisciplinary approach leads students to recognize different human values as they are expressed in the world's literature, visual art, music, philosophy, and religion.

The Department of Natural Science offers a series of courses designed to help students develop a scientific grasp of their environment and their relationship to it. The need for international understanding and cooperation to bring about solutions to global problems is stressed.

These programs were designed to complement each other. The departments have 32 faculty and enroll about 7,500 each year. Funding is provided entirely by the university. Eastern also has a major in Ibero-American studies and participates with other regional universities in offering study-abroad programs.

HOW ORGANIZED. EKU has nine colleges. Most students are required to take 46 hours of general education courses, which are distributed among 5 areas: symbolics of information, humanities, social science, natural science, and physical education. Most departments within the university have a number of offerings that have been approved as general education courses. Many courses approved for general education in the social sciences, the humanities, and the natural sciences have global emphases. Each department has a chairperson and an operating budget that includes faculty salaries, educational supplies, and other expenses. Student evaluations are required of all faculty.

The department chairmen are responsible for conducting the three interdisciplinary programs. Faculty committees advise on content and review, and each program's curriculum is supervised by the dean of the college in which the department is located.

EDUCATIONAL IMPACT. Eastern's effort to link general education with interdisciplinary global education has made faculty more aware that today's complex problems cannot be adequately understood or analyzed from the perspective of a single cultural tradition or a single discipline. An interdisciplinary faculty has been developed and efforts have been made to establish communication among faculty in traditional departments. With team teaching in some general education classes, faculty are working together to refine the interdisciplinary global framework. One other measure of the endeavor's impact is that an honors program and a capstone course with international and global emphases are being considered.

RESOURCE PERSON. Kenneth R. Nelson, Roark 105, Eastern Kentucky University, Richmond, KY 40475. Phone: (606) 622-2565.

A full-length description of Earlham College, which pioneered an integrated curriculum model of intercultural studies, is found in The Role of the Scholarly Disciplines, *Change Magazine Press, 1980; E&WV Series I.*

ECKERD COLLEGE, St. Petersburg, FL

Eckerd College, founded in 1958 as Florida Presbyterian College, is now related by covenant to the Presbyterian Church, U.S., and the United Presbyterian Church, U.S.A. The name was changed in 1972 to recognize the generosity of Jack M. Eckerd, a Florida civic leader and businessman. Eckerd has a student body of 1,100 with approximately 10 percent coming from outside the continental United States, representing more than 30 countries. It has 65 full-time faculty and another 8 full-time equivalent positions; 82 percent have doctoral degrees. The college's annual budget is $9.2 million and it has an endowment of $3.6 million. About 57 percent of Eckerd freshmen graduate, and 50 percent of graduates continue to study for advanced degrees.

INTERNATIONAL ASPECTS OF THE CURRICULUM. Eckerd College has a tradition of emphasis on international education. For the first ten years of the college's existence, all students were required to complete a three-year sequence in a language and two courses in East Asian studies. A significant majority of those early graduates also participated in international education programs abroad sponsored by the college. In 1971 the language requirement was dropped, but the emphasis on understanding other cultures was continued in the general education program through a World View requirement, with options in area studies, cross-cultural single-discipline courses, and language study. Opportunities for studying outside the United States continued to be provided with semester programs at Eckerd's own centers in London and Florence, in cooperative programs in France, Spain, Colombia, and Germany, and with Winter Terms scheduled regularly in England, Ireland, Scandinavia, Spain, Mexico, Germany, the Soviet Union, and on several Caribbean islands.

In 1973 the faculty structure was reorganized from three academic divisions into five collegia. The Collegium of Comparative Cultures was assigned to coordinate language instruction, area studies majors, and study-abroad programs. A second charge to the collegium was to design a series of area studies courses to serve as the sophomore year of the four-year general education program. About 7 percent of students are affiliated with the Collegium of Comparative Cultures, but virtually every student comes into contact with the area studies and/or language program of the collegium in meeting the World View requirement.

The Collegium of Comparative Cultures operates on a nonsalary budget of approximately $7,000 for its on-campus programs. The International Education Office works with faculty from all five collegia to provide overseas opportunities for all students.

HOW ORGANIZED. About half the faculty in the Comparative Cultures Collegium are language instructors; other disciplines represented include anthropology, history, philosophy, and religion. These faculty, with cooperation from other disciplines, staff interdisciplinary courses in East Asian, Soviet, Latin-American, French, German, Spanish, and African area studies which meet the World View requirement for sophomores. They also teach special cross-cultural courses for juniors and seniors which serve as options in the Values Sequences curriculum.

Each area studies course has a printed syllabus with course objectives, readings and written assignments, and evaluation criteria. Teaching approaches vary, but an integral part of each area studies course is an examination of the values inherent in the foreign culture, compared with those of our own. Each course is evaluated by students.

Language instruction resides primarily in the Collegium of Comparative Cultures. Two courses in a single language beyond the elementary level are considered equivalent to an area studies course in fulfilling the World View requirement. In 1979 a select group of single-discipline courses from the behavioral sciences and the letters collegia were also approved as area studies equivalents. A total of two area studies courses, or equivalents, is required for all students.

EDUCATIONAL IMPACT. International education has been an important part of the Eckerd curriculum from the very beginning, and it continues to receive strong support from faculty. A recent survey found 62 percent expressing a desire to reinstitute a language requirement, and a curriculum reform committee recently advocated a required international or intercultural experience for all students, in addition to a World View requirement. One indication of real faculty support for the international education program is the fact that 65 percent of all faculty that have been at the college for at least three years have participated in Eckerd Winter Term, semester, or summer programs abroad. About 55 percent of Eckerd graduates have taken these programs.

RESOURCE PERSON. William H. Parsons, Eckerd College, PO Box 12560, St. Petersburg, FL 33733. Phone: (813) 867-1166, x274/231.

EISENHOWER COLLEGE OF ROCHESTER INSTITUTE OF TECHNOLOGY, Seneca Falls, NY

Chartered in 1965 and opened in 1968, Eisenhower is a private liberal arts college. In 1968, by an act of Congress, it was designated as a memorial to President Dwight David Eisenhower. In March 1979 Eisenhower became the tenth college of Rochester Institute of Technology, a 150-year-old private institution geared to career-oriented education. Eisenhower has 560 undergraduates in 7 interdisciplinary degree programs—community services, economics, environmental studies, humanities, interdisciplinary science, international relations, and public policy. The college has 43 full-time and 13 part-time faculty; 72 percent have doctoral degrees. Approximately 40 percent of Eisenhower graduates have gone on to graduate study.

INTERNATIONAL ASPECTS OF THE CURRICULUM. From the outset the *World Studies Program* has been the centerpiece of Eisenhower's general education program. A required 3-year core curriculum of 32 semester hours, it organizes the college's institutional life in a way that provides intellectual and social experiences guiding students in their development of a global perspective.

The program is interdisciplinary; it is staffed by faculty from the humanities, political science, economics, sociology, anthropology, and the sciences. The material requires both faculty and students to coordinate the essential modes of thinking in all these disciplines in order to analyze historical and contemporary world issues. The student is forced to think beyond the confines of a single discipline and to synthesize numerous factors before making value judgments and proposing solutions. The program is also fully international, treating Eastern and Third World (as well as Western) societies in some depth.

Each of the three years of study involves a separate approach. The first year (12 semester hours) is an area studies introduction to Major Cultural Traditions and Major Culture Areas of the World. The second year (also 12 semester hours) is a historical treatment of Modern World History From 1700 to the Present. The third year (8 semester hours, taken by junior-year-abroad students in their senior year) is a problems approach that treats Contemporary Issues and Perspectives in Science/Technology and in Society/The Arts.

HOW ORGANIZED. Eisenhower's World Studies Program is directed by the associate dean for academic affairs. The U.S. Department of Education has funded a Center for World Studies at the college; this means that the functions of director of the center and of the program have been performed by the same person. It is the mission of the Center for World Studies to support language and other activities associated with the World Studies Program. It also aims to make available to area educators the expertise and resources developed during 12 years of experience with this World Studies curriculum.

In the program itself, however, each semester's courses are under the direction of a single faculty coordinator who works with a faculty team to present, coordinate, and evaluate the lectures and discussion sessions of each interdisciplinary, team-taught course. Most overall planning is done by these teams during month-long summer workshops, where course materials are selected—and at times developed—by the faculty.

EDUCATIONAL IMPACT. Because the World Studies Program involves more than half the Eisenhower staff—faculty from virtually every degree program —the interdisciplinary and international approach has heavily affected faculty appointments and curricular development outside of general education. Eisenhower is now transforming all its degree programs into interdisciplinary ones (decided in 1979), and many (such as international relations, economics, environmental studies, public policy, and humanities) have a clear global dimension.

The program has stimulated educational experiences abroad for faculty and students during the January term; a Department of Education-funded six-week trip to Egypt by 16 World Studies faculty was developed as a part of program planning; and World Studies faculty contributed to the development of the Educational Testing Service "Survey of Global Understanding" (which the college now gives to students beginning and finishing the World Studies Program). Recognition of the program has transformed a small, rural college into a genuine center for world studies, both for its own students and faculty and for other educators in the area.

RESOURCE PERSON. David D. Murdoch, Eisenhower College of Rochester Institute of Technology, Seneca Falls, NY 13148. Phone: (315) 568-7475.

EMORY UNIVERSITY, Atlanta, GA

Emory College was founded in 1836 in Oxford, Georgia, and moved in 1915 to Atlanta. It is the coeducational undergraduate arts and sciences school of Emory University. Its fall 1980 enrollment was 3,016. Emory University has professional schools of business, dentistry, law, medicine, nursing, and theology; an arts and sciences graduate school; and a two-year college on the original campus at Oxford. Enrollment in the rest of the university is 4,916. It has 206 full-time faculty, of which 98 percent have doctorates. The annual budget of Emory College (includes Graduate School of Arts and Sciences and Candler and Woodruff libraries) is $19.2 million. The university has an endowment of $212 million. More than 70 percent of Emory College graduates continue in professional and other postgraduate study.

INTERNATIONAL ASPECTS OF THE CURRICULUM. The *Emory Program in International Studies* (EPIS) is neither degree conferring nor a department in its own right. It exists to stimulate international studies. EPIS sponsors lectures and programs, provides summer stipends for faculty to develop new courses, and publishes a monthly newsletter. More than 80 courses are offered through EPIS by 8 different departments in the areas of the Middle East, China, Latin America, Europe, and international relations. The approach is interdisciplinary. Most of the courses offered by EPIS during its first year were already established before the program began, but 23 were designed by 8 faculty members who received EPIS stipends in the previous summer. Another eight grants for course development were made for the second summer of the program. Courses are designed by specialists in a number of disciplines: religion, sociology, history, political science, Romance languages, theology, and anthropology.

Emory's language department offers a basic two-year program in Hebrew, Arabic, and Italian, with more comprehensive programs in German, Russian, Greek, Latin, French, and Spanish. The latter two are available in a doctoral program as well. The interest in language studies is growing, and the presence of EPIS is expected to generate further participation. A symbiotic relationship exists between language study and international studies; language students now seek courses offered through EPIS in order to broaden their experiences.

Emory's Summer Study Abroad Programs, operating since 1973, have attracted steadily increasing numbers of participants, reaching a record 136 students in summer 1980. For summer 1981 Emory has designed 8 programs in 5 countries.

EPIS special presentations have attracted greater attention and reached more students. EPIS offered 66 presentations in its first year and a half, including a German film festival, luncheon speakers every other week, faculty seminars, a conference on world terrorism, and a contemporary lecture series. The events were attended by a total of 4,761; of these 1,200 signed up to receive the EPIS newsletter.

HOW ORGANIZED. EPIS was launched in July 1979 with a $36,000 Department (then Office) of Education grant; another $36,000 was approved for 1980-81. Over the next two years $250,704 will be spent to implement the program; Emory's contribution is 70 percent of the estimated cost. Not included in Emory's forecast contribution are the salaries of faculty who have developed the new or revised courses or the annual $250,000 expenditure for library acquisitions in international, global, or area studies. A Middle East expert works half time as director and teaches half time. There is also a three-fourths-time program coordinator and newsletter editor as well as a half-time secretary-assistant. At regular intervals the effectiveness of the program's activities is evaluated.

EPIS contributes to the fulfillment of point nine of the undergraduate curricular objectives passed by the faculty in October 1976: "Knowledge of a culture other than one's own." EPIS is expected to have a major effect on the undergraduate curriculum over the next decade.

EDUCATIONAL IMPACT. There is a consensus among faculty, students, and staff that the launching and institutionalization of EPIS has been successful. EPIS programs, lectures, conferences, special cultural events, course development, faculty seminars, and luncheon meetings have provided a global perspective and a better understanding of internationally related problems and issues. Students and faculty have shown increased interest for the new course offerings. The administration has been enthusiastic and supportive. Also, the Atlanta community has eagerly participated and benefited from EPIS-sponsored activities and programs. It is estimated that approximately two thirds of undergraduates have been affected by EPIS's special course offerings and presentations.

RESOURCE PERSON. Kenneth W. Stein, Director, Emory Program in International Studies, 109-A History Building, Emory University, Atlanta, GA 30322. Phone: (404) 329-6562.

GEORGETOWN UNIVERSITY, Washington, DC

Georgetown University has been located in the nation's capital since the founding of Georgetown College in 1789. The Jesuit institution's 5,400 undergraduates, 6,200 graduate students, and 935 full-time faculty comprise an interdenominational and coeducational community. The university consists of five undergraduate schools—arts and sciences (1789), nursing (1903), foreign service (1919), languages and linguistics (1949), and business administration (1956); four graduate and professional schools—graduate (1820), medicine (1851), law (1870), and dentistry (1899); and the School for Summer and Continuing Education (1954). The university's Center for Strategic and International Studies conducts research and issues publications on subjects of public policy and international affairs. Georgetown's $206 million annual budget is supported by a $60 million endowment.

INTERNATIONAL ASPECTS OF THE CURRICULUM. Georgetown University's *Edmund A. Walsh School of Foreign Service* is the oldest school of international affairs in the United States and the largest in the world. At the undergraduate level the school offers a four-year, multidisciplinary, professionally oriented liberal arts program in international affairs to 1,250 students, 23 percent of the university's undergraduates, leading to the BS in foreign service. The student population, one fourth of whom have lived abroad prior to matriculation, is half male and half female, 10 percent minority, and 10 percent foreign national. Students apply directly to the school, which has its own administration, a full-time faculty of 20, 60 associate faculty from other university departments, and 40 adjunct faculty in specialized fields, drawn from the private and public sectors in Washington, D.C. The school offers more than 100 courses annually and also draws on courses from 24 departments throughout the university. An annual budget of $5 million is supported through general university revenues, supplemented by external fund raising averaging $500,000 annually.

All students complete a required core of study in the freshman and sophomore years: modern foreign language; two years of internationally oriented study in economics, government, and history; one year of study in English, philosophy, and theology; and one semester in an internationally oriented Sophomore Seminar. Juniors and seniors pursue one of the following divisions of study: History and Diplomacy, International Politics, International Economics, Comparative and Regional Studies, and the Humanities in International Affairs.

Graduation from the school is based on an oral and a reading examination in a modern language, ten of which are offered by Georgetown's School of Languages and Linguistics. The school encourages students to study abroad through direct matriculation in a recognized institution. In recent years 40 percent of the school's undergraduates have studied in 44 countries in partial fulfillment of their degree requirements. In conjunction with their upperclass divisions, students may participate in Certificate Programs offered by the school's programs in African Studies, Asian Studies, Contemporary Arab Studies, German Public and International Affairs, and International Business Diplomacy. A Senior Honors Program, consisting of year-long, internationally oriented research seminars, is conducted for those who have received honors-level evaluations throughout their undergraduate studies. Students obtaining jobs or internships in the Washington area may earn academic credit through independent research projects.

HOW ORGANIZED. The School of Foreign Service undergraduate program is administered by a dean, an associate dean, two assistant deans, and a professional staff. Governance is provided by an executive council and committees composed of faculty, students, and administration which establish policy and review all aspects of the school's academic program, including admissions, curriculum, and standards. The school develops curricular offerings for permanent location in academic departments, and international academic offerings throughout the university are reviewed annually for inclusion in its curriculum. Advising of students is conducted by faculty, administration, foreign affairs professionals, and selected upperclass students. Administrative functions of admissions, alumni affairs, development, financial aid, foreign study, placement, and records are provided through direct collaboration with central university offices.

The school sponsors in its Washington location lecture series, seminars, symposia, and panels on subjects of international significance, as well as developing internship and placement opportunities. The school's development efforts have focused on the creation of institutes and programs in African Studies, Asian Studies, Contemporary Arab Studies, Diplomacy, German Public and International Affairs, and International Business Diplomacy, which relate the school to Washington, national, and international resources and contribute to its teaching, advising, and fund-raising functions. The school involves professionals in many phases of international endeavor in its program and administration.

EDUCATIONAL IMPACT. The School of Foreign Service provides the primary focus for Georgetown University's international outlook and involvement. It is the central university point for the development of international programs, curricula, and fund raising. Because of its size and because it conducts one of the university's largest master's programs, the school provides the resources that encourage and make feasible internationally related offerings throughout the university. It includes in its activities faculty and students with international interests regardless of their departmental or school affiliation. The school has been central in the conception and development of the university's new Intercultural Center; as of 1982 it will house the School of Foreign Service, its associated programs, and other international activities of the university.

RESOURCE PERSON. Matthew M. Gardner, Jr., Associate Dean, School of Foreign Service, Georgetown University, Washington, DC 20057. Phone: (202) 625-4218.

GOSHEN COLLEGE, Goshen, IN

Founded in 1894 as a preparatory school in Elkhart, Indiana, Goshen College began offering college courses in 1903 when it was moved to Goshen. Since 1969 it has been solely a four-year coeducational liberal arts college, owned and operated by the Mennonite Church. The college offers the BA in 33 areas and the BS in nursing. Goshen's more than 1,200 students come from 38 states, 4 Canadian provinces, and 36 countries. Because of the emphasis on service, many students choose majors such as nursing, education, social work, and business. About 75 percent are Mennonites; the rest represent a wide variety of faiths and cultures. The faculty has 77 full-time and 36 part-time members; 71 percent of full-time faculty hold doctorates. A majority also have international experience through study and church-related service, and most speak more than one language. The college's 1980-81 budget is projected at $8.4 million; it has completed the past 42 fiscal years without a budget deficit.

INTERNATIONAL ASPECTS OF THE CURRICULUM. The core of Goshen's international education program is the *Study-Service Trimester* (SST), whose primary objectives are to help students examine and experience the culture of a developing or significantly different country; serve in a practical way by participating in a program or project in close contact with local persons; experience an intensive relationship as part of a small group with one or two faculty members; and contribute to a climate of international understanding and interest on the Goshen campus.

Since SST began in 1968, more than 3,000 students (an average of 245 per year) have lived and studied in other countries, mostly those of the Third World. SST units have been operated in Belize, Costa Rica, El Salvador, Guadeloupe, Haiti, Honduras, Jamaica, and Nicaragua at the same cost to the student as a trimester in residence on campus. Special units bearing extra charges (because of longer travel) have been held in Germany, South Korea, and Poland. In 1980 SST initiated the first undergraduate exchange program with the People's Republic of China. A new German studies unit will be conducted in East and West Germany in spring 1981.

The SST experience is interdisciplinary, with an emphasis on experiential education and service. Usually led by a faculty couple, each SST unit of approximately 20 students spends the first 7 weeks of the 14-week term studying the language and culture of the host country. During the second part of the trimester, students disperse to various parts of the country to work in service projects, linked where possible to the student's major field and usually supervised by a local citizen. Assignments include work as teaching assistants, health service aides, playground supervisors, or construction helpers. Students live with local families.

SST is part of Goshen's general education program and the off-campus term or an equivalent set of on-campus courses is required for graduation. Students are eligible for the program after two trimesters in residence on campus; most elect to take it during the sophomore year. Since the program's beginning more than 80 percent of eligible students have chosen SST. Prerequisites include the equivalent of two college courses in the language of the host country. Students also undergo medical and psychological screening before participating.

The SST program is administered by the college's division of international education, which consists of two full-time faculty and two who teach part time with other departments. The international education division also coordinates Goshen's study and work programs in Poland and Haiti, several courses per year taught abroad, and the college's program for international students.

HOW ORGANIZED. All Goshen faculty may apply as SST leaders; they are selected jointly by the president, provost, dean, and director of international education. Typically, faculty go abroad for a full year. Most leaders spend several months on location studying the language before the school year starts. An overlap with the previous leader is made in continuing units. Faculty orientation is completed on campus.

Since faculty leaders from SST are chosen from all departments (including administrative divisions), specific curricula during the study portion of SST differ from location to location and from year to year. Most study programs feature guest lectures by national experts in areas such as politics, geography and ecology, the arts, and social customs; field trips; readings; and the student's keeping of a journal. The language study component also remains fairly constant from year to year, as this is usually administered by a national language school.

The SST program has undergone extensive evaluation twice: by an outside team of international education experts and by a committee of college, community, and Mennonite Church representatives. The former group concluded that "most students derived great value from the SST experience.... The program is an imaginative one, thoughtfully designed and administered, and has rendered a signal contribution to the total educational enterprise at Goshen College."

Funding for SST is carried out through the normal fee structures of the college. This is possible because the program is operated at about the same cost as that for an equal number of students on campus.

EDUCATIONAL IMPACT. The primary SST goal is "to contribute to a climate of international understanding and interest on the Goshen College campus." All students, faculty, and alumni have reported broader awareness of world needs, intercultural understanding and sensitivity, and greater self-reliance. Faculty believe that SST broadens one's world, develops an awareness of Third World needs, helps participants understand cultural differences, and stimulates coping skills and personal growth.

Goshen College has always reflected the Mennonite Church's tradition of international understanding; the SST program has brought a special clarity to that tradition. Courses are taught with more international perspectives and students show a greater interest in issues and people beyond their home environments.

RESOURCE PERSON. Arlin Hunsberger, Director of International Education, Goshen College, Goshen, IN 46526. Phone: (219) 533-3161, x256.

GOUCHER COLLEGE, Towson, MD

Goucher is a private liberal arts institution on the north side of Baltimore. Founded in 1885, it has been committed to quality liberal arts education for women. About 1,000 undergraduates are enrolled. There are also a master of arts program in dance-movement therapy and a program for returning women for the bachelor's degree. There are 15 departments and a variety of interdepartmental programs offering majors in fields such as women's studies, area studies, and premed and prelegal. The Julia Rodgers Library has 220,000 volumes and Goucher's endowment exceeds $18 million.

INTERNATIONAL ASPECTS OF THE CURRICULUM. The primary program for global studies is the *international relations (IR)* major. It is interdisciplinary, drawing on the departments of political science, economics, history, modern languages, and behavioral sciences (anthropology and sociology, communication, and psychology). The major emphasizes analytic skills, substantive knowledge, and language competency necessary for careers with international organizations, government, or international business. It also prepares students for master's programs in international affairs. Students interested in pursuing the PhD and careers in teaching and research are encouraged to study international relations within a political science major.

A student majoring in IR selects at least 12 courses from the disciplines constituting the major. This is done in consultation with the director of the international relations program. The precise mix of courses depends on each student's interests and career concerns, e.g., the desire to develop a business background or a specialty in a geographic region. Beyond introductory courses in political science, history, and economics, courses in international relations theory, comparative political analysis, and international economics are needed for the major. Proficiency in a language is required through at least the intermediate level. Languages taught include Arabic, French, German, Russian, and Spanish. These courses also address the broader area studies considerations of a region's culture, society, and politics. The typical IR major involves a series of more analytic political science courses, a focus on a region (e.g., East Asia, the Soviet Union, Europe, Latin America) which includes historical and sociological dimensions, intermediate macro- and microeconomics along with international economics, and one language pursued through the senior year to the advanced level.

Goucher students are encouraged to take advantage of a number of curriculum-related activities. These include study abroad during the junior year, participation in interuniversity conferences, a Model UN, and an international internship in government, business, or an organization.

HOW ORGANIZED. The program is directed by the political science professor specializing in international politics, who works with a committee of representatives from the relevant departments. This committee deals with long-term matters such as curriculum design and course content. The director manages the program on a day-by-day basis, advises the international relations majors, organizes all program activities, and supervises international internships.

Since it is an interdepartmental program there is no separate budgetary allocation. Any funding is included in the political science department's budget, though ad hoc funding for special activities or lecturers comes from the office of the dean. The program draws almost entirely on existing resources and offerings from the departments. In fact, it requires minimal financial commitment.

EDUCATIONAL IMPACT. International relations is a growing field at Goucher. There are more than 40 majors, an 800 percent increase over the last 4 years. One benefit has been increased cross-departmental cooperation among faculty. Although the program director is the principal teacher of international politics courses—ranging from IR theory and comparative foreign policy to U.S.-Soviet relations and the politics of global economic relations—use of the Interdepartmental Committee and colleagues in other disciplines ensures adequate breadth of content for the IR program. Thus the multidisciplinary format enhanced the teaching of international elements in many other courses. Further, the opportunity to undertake double majors or at least an IR concentration in addition to one's major has drawn more students to international courses, a fact not lost on an administration confronting the enrollment problems of the 1980s.

RESOURCE PERSON. Joe D. Hagan, Chairman, International Relations Program, Goucher College, Towson, MD 21204. Phone: (301) 825-3300, x304.

HAMPTON INSTITUTE, Hampton, VA

Hampton Institute, founded in 1868 by General Samuel Chapman for the education of black freedmen, is a coeducational, nondenominational private college. It enrolls approximately 3,000 students who represent 35 states and 17 countries. The faculty numbers about 210; 40 percent hold doctorates. Hampton offers 39 baccalaureate degrees, plus master's degrees in 9 fields. The academic areas are: School of Education, School of Arts and Letters, School of Pure and Applied Sciences, School of Business, and School of Nursing. Five buildings on campus have been listed in the National Register of Historic Landmarks.

INTERNATIONAL ASPECTS OF THE CURRICULUM. During 1979-80 the Studies Area in Modern Foreign Languages at Hampton Institute, with the collaboration of four other colleges and universities of black heritage, infused curriculum materials based on the cultures of the francophone and hispanophone African Diaspora and continental Africa into beginning French and Spanish courses. Through this approach the *African Cultural Elements in Language Learning (AFCELL)*, teachers can offer cultural and linguistic links with French- and Spanish-speaking black peoples of the world. It is perceived as a means of stimulating interest in languages while extending ethnic identity to languages and literatures. The student is also exposed to international and cross-cultural perspectives through the study of Third World peoples. This development project was funded by the National Endowment for the Humanities.

Language professors at Hampton Institute, Howard University, the University of the District of Columbia, Morgan State University, and Morehouse College engaged in this informal consortium of curriculum development and teaching. At a summer workshop potential teachers, along with consultants in literature, history, art, music, anthropology, and language education, developed instructional modules or learning packets in the following areas: geography and demography; sociohistorical; cultural performing arts; and introduction to literature. Eight French and seven Spanish modules were written and taught. The French modules are: L'Afrique francophone noire: geographie politique; L'Afrique francophone noire: aspects divers; Les Antilles françaises: vue d'ensemble; Une Famille senegalaise; Un Conte antillais: ''Pe Tambou a''; ''Choucoune'': meringue haitienne; Un Conte africain: ''Le Taureau de Bouki'' (adaptation); and La Peinture haitienne—expression vivante d'une culture. The Spanish modules are: Las regiones negras en Hispanoamerica; El Negro en Hispanoamerica; Los reinos negros en la epoca colonial; La Santeria; La Influencia africana en la musica latinoamericana; ''Hermano Negro''—poema; Un cuento, ''Dos Caminos'' por Quince Duncan. A major goal is to produce modules in the form of learning kits by a commercial publisher. A prototype kit of the French module Un Conte africain: ''Le Taureau de Bouki'' has been developed.

HOW ORGANIZED. Hampton Institute distributed printed materials to the participating colleges. Three to four modules were infused each semester into regular first-year French and Spanish courses at the other institutions. Teachers have been encouraged to instruct in the target language. Students are given a pretest to determine general knowledge. All modules contain an overview that states student objectives and learning and evaluation activities. The presentation of the written cultural text is accompanied by specially prepared visuals (slides, transparencies, photographs, etc.) when available. Included are exercises for oral and writing practice. Finally, a posttest is administered.

The student is asked to complete a Student Attitude Toward Module form after meeting module requirements; this is part of the evaluation process. Other types of evaluation are validation of modules prior to field testing; monitoring of field testing sites by project director; evaluation of all project activities by an external evaluator from a major midwest university.

In the current academic year the modules have been institutionalized and taught at three of the colleges mentioned above and at two others that asked to participate.

In January 1980 the project director made an exploratory trip to Martinique and Guadeloupe and to certain areas populated by blacks in Venezuela and Colombia. Rare materials were acquired for the project and local links were established or renewed. Pictures were taken from which 250 slides have been developed for potential use in the modular program.

EDUCATIONAL IMPACT. AFCELL has been well accepted at Hampton Institute. The administration has supported its activities and is furnishing internal funds. Language teachers involved in the program have contributed enthusiastically to its progress. Faculty from other disciplines, such as ethnic studies, music, art, history, and political science, have joined various activities, including interdisciplinary teaching. Evaluation of several project components indicates that students enjoy and benefit from the cultural elements in the language courses. AFCELL activities have been positively received by professional journals and at workshops and conferences. The future for expansion of the program generally is unlimited, particularly with regard to enhancing global and international perspectives. Hampton Institute is applying for a three-year grant from the National Endowment for the Humanities to continue this work.

RESOURCE PERSON. Beatrice Stith Clark, Hampton Institute, PO Box 6253, Hampton, VA 23668. Phone: (804) 727-5679.

HOOD COLLEGE, Frederick, MD

Founded in 1893, Hood is a four-year liberal arts college for women. It has 1,097 undergraduates and 607 part-time graduate students enrolled in master's programs. There are 32 major areas leading to the BA degree, 3 leading to the BS. The coeducational graduate school has 10 graduate programs leading to the MA degree and 3 leading to the MS. The college has 94 full-time and 67 part-time faculty; 60 percent of full-time staff have doctorates; the average age of the faculty is 40. The college's annual budget is $8.2 million and the endowment is $8 million. Sixty-three percent of all Hood freshmen graduate, of which thirty-seven percent continue in postbaccalaureate education.

INTERNATIONAL ASPECTS OF THE CURRICULUM. The international dimension of Hood College's curriculum has three components: a structured interdepartmental major in Latin-American studies that requires a junior year in a Latin-American country; Hood's Junior Year at Strasbourg University (since 1967); affiliation with Sevilla and Cadiz programs of the Council on International Educational Exchange; and an internship site at Koler, Germany.

A strong language program that offers—besides the traditional language courses leading to teaching or graduate studies—an introduction to translation and interpretation, vocabulary development for the world of work, and cross-cultural courses, thereby providing skills and background for careers in government, business, and international organizations requiring bilingual training. Hood students may live in the French, German, or Spanish Houses, where residents speak the language at all times. A young native speaker is in residence to promote the cultural atmosphere and activities that make each house a miniature "other world." The most popular activities sponsored by the houses are the language dining tables, the Oktoberfest, the International Christmas Party, and the Mardi Gras. Lectures, films, and field trips of an international nature are also offered.

A choice of an interdepartmental major designed by the student with the help of a faculty committee, a double major, or a certificate of proficiency to combine any area of specialization with languages and foreign studies. Recently students have combined a language with Mathematics and Computer Science, Communications, Sociology, Management and Economics, Psychology, Political Science, and Recreation and Leisure Studies. The Department of Foreign Languages places students as interns in international organizations and government or in private agencies where languages and cross-cultural understanding are required. Some that have provided valuable experiences have been the Mexican embassy, French television, the French embassy (Office of Cultural Affairs and Commercial Office), Ayuda, Organization of American States (Department of Scientific Affairs, Commission on Human Rights, Interamerican Commission of Women), the Committee of Spanish-Speaking Community of Virginia, the Alliance Francaise, Servicios Industriales Peñoles in Mexico City, and General Motors of Strasbourg, France. Hood's Junior Year at Strasbourg is the only program in Strasbourg offering internships. There is a separate budget for the junior year program in Strasbourg; other components are handled through the budgets of the departments involved.

HOW ORGANIZED. The first two components work as in other four-year colleges. The Latin-American studies major, under the auspices of the foreign language department, includes, in addition to courses in Spanish language and literature, appropriate courses in anthropology, art, economics, geography, history, sociology, and political science. Hood's double and interdepartmental majors, as well as the certificate of proficiency in French/German/Spanish, maximize resources and provide a sound international perspective.

Students must fulfill requirements in both fields for a double major, with a faculty advisor from each one. No more than 90 credits in the combined majors are allowed toward the 124 credit hours required for graduation. There is a trend toward double majors. Combination of a language with history, management, psychology, political science, and recreation are in great demand.

Students may design their own interdepartmental major focusing on courses from two or more related disciplines. Students select a program advisory committee made up of faculty advisors in each of the fields to be included in the program. The primary advisor is chosen for the field in which the student plans to acquire the greatest expertise. A minimum of 15 credit hours in one of the areas represented in the major and 12 credit hours in another field is required. Remaining credit hours must total a minimum of 36 and a maximum of 60.

A certificate of proficiency requires a minimum of 15 credits beyond the intermediate level, plus an oral and a written exam. Students have official statements recorded on their transcripts. This original Hood idea has been adopted by other colleges in the area.

Programs are evaluated through institutional research and reassessed each year on Planning Day. Courses are evaluated at the departmental level. The Strasbourg program conducts midyear and end-of-year evaluations. All international programs have been approved by the faculty as permanent offerings.

EDUCATIONAL IMPACT. Hood's interdepartmental majors are successful because faculty are willing to transcend the limitations of their fields.

The language houses, the presence of different language assistants every year, and the return of fluent and internationally aware students from a year of study abroad have made the Hood campus keenly aware of and receptive to other cultures and languages. A new core curriculum to be implemented in fall 1981 requires a language component and a world culture category.

The flexibility of the majors offered and the fact that any combination can be initiated by a student or by a department affords infinite possibilities. Departments have been very cooperative in helping students achieve their goals. A number of home economics majors have spent a semester in Spain, France, or Germany working for a certificate of proficiency. Several management majors have fulfilled the internship requirement while abroad; at home, other internships, such as those of Ayuda and TESS, have combined sociology with Spanish. The positive attitude of the college community is reflected in the fact that the Department of Management and Economics recommends attainment of a certificate of proficiency in a language; the Department of Sociology and Social Work advises students to earn a certificate of proficiency in Spanish; and the Department of Mathematics and Computer Science is working on an interdepartmental major combining computer expertise with language proficiency.

RESOURCE PERSON. Juana Hernandez, Chairperson, Department of Foreign Languages and Literatures, Hood College, Frederick, MD 21701. Phone: (301) 663-3131, x258/244.

JOHNSON COUNTY COMMUNITY COLLEGE
Overland Park, KS

Since opening in 1969, Johnson County Community College (JCCC) has been a two-year public college receiving financial support from Kansas and from Johnson County. Located within the seven-county area designated as the Kansas City Standard Metropolitan Statistical Area, JCCC is a comprehensive, open-door community college, providing and facilitating equal educational opportunities, with a commitment to lifelong learning and the idea that everyone in the community is part of its student body. In 1980 there were 6,375 credit students and 6,219 noncredit students in the continuing education program. There are 136 full-time and 150 part-time faculty. The average faculty age is 38.

INTERNATIONAL ASPECTS OF THE CURRICULUM. The college has taken an integrated, comprehensive approach to international education. In the first year of an endeavor to provide the opportunity for international experiences to all students, staff, and many from the community, the program has three parts. First, eight teaching modules are being developed on East Asia and eight on Latin America—on urban and population problems, the concept of individuality in Asian culture, examination of race prejudice in Latin America, views of the U.S. in Latin America, the role of religion in different societies. The modules are multifunctional, with some integrated into the existing curriculum and others used as independent study courses or as part of the noncredit continuing education program. Second, new international courses are being offered: videotaped self-paced study in Chinese and Japanese designed to prepare students for more advanced course work at other institutions; Eastern civilizations; Latin-American civilizations, ideology, nationalism (Communism in China, Cuba, and the USSR). Third, a year-long staff development colloquium has been designed to help faculty give international focuses to courses already offered in the curriculum.

The first annual budget is $83,162. Courses and modules ready for spring 1981 will be integrated into the curriculum and into existing courses, or used as independent study programs; some courses will be offered as part of the noncredit community service program, while others will be offered this way and as a part of the regular curriculum.

HOW ORGANIZED. The international education program is headed by the director of continuing education/international education, who devotes half time to the program and is assisted by a half-time program assistant. The director is advised by an International Education Task Force composed of interested faculty members from every division at JCCC. At present 40 percent of the program is funded through outside sources. The intention is to make the program independent of this support (except for special projects) within three years and to establish it permanently in the regular curriculum. The goal is to diffuse international education throughout the entire curriculum. Membership in the International Student Exchange Program enables students to study abroad one year at selected foreign universities at nominal cost. JCCC monitors progress through curriculum and instruction surveys, in which both faculty and students participate. Also, a survey instrument is used to measure students' international awareness.

Arrangements with two sister colleges in Taiwan and faculty exchanges with these institutions have enhanced faculty and student interest in international education. The college also participates in the International/Intercultural Consortium of the American Association of Community and Junior Colleges, which has a wide range of programs that further international dimensions at JCCC.

EDUCATIONAL IMPACT. The program has caused both faculty and administration to think across division lines and blur the distinctions between career and academic education. It has forced JCCC to think of the world and the student as a whole and has thrown the institution and its people back onto their own resources. JCCC is pleasantly surprised to find that it is creating course modules and new courses that reflect world complexities. This has stimulated faculty to examine the entire curriculum with a view to wholesale reordering of perspective. The programs have also aroused student interest and introduced a cosmopolitan outlook not evident one or two years ago.

RESOURCE PERSON. Robert Demeritt, Director, International Education/Continuing Education or Lewis Bernstein, Program Assistant, International Education Program, Johnson County Community College, College Boulevard and Quivira Road, Overland Park, KS 66210. Phone: (913) 677-8590.

KALAMAZOO COLLEGE, Kalamazoo, MI

Kalamazoo is a private, coeducational, church-related liberal arts college. Founded in 1833, it is the oldest institution of higher learning in Michigan. A year-round curriculum was introduced in 1961. Known as the K Plan, it combines foreign study, career development, and an individualized research project off campus with academic offerings, cocurricular activities, and residential living experiences on campus. A 92-member faculty provides a traditional liberal arts curriculum enhanced by American studies, African studies, public policy studies, women's studies, and international commerce for 1,450 students. The annual budget is $10.6 million with an endowment of $13.6 million.

INTERNATIONAL ASPECTS OF THE CURRICULUM. The *Foreign Study Program* provides the backbone for Kalamazoo's international focus. About 85 percent of graduates select a one-, two-, or three-quarter foreign study experience. The goals for foreign study are: to become acquainted in some depth with a culture (usually including language), a people, and an educational system different from one's own; and to participate in an academic experience that is comparable in quality to campus work and significantly enriched by the environment in which it takes place. Participants not only benefit academically, but return with an increased understanding of themselves and their own country as well as the country visited.

Proficiency in a second language, required for most foreign study programs, provides strong support for the on-campus language offerings and language graduation requirement. Programs, including some fully integrated into foreign universities, have been designed to make different kinds of linguistic demands on participants. The program of self-instruction in less commonly taught languages, pioneered at Kalamazoo in the 1960s, continues to add a further dimension to major concentrations in French, German, and Spanish.

Strong ties with a number of universities in Anglo- and Francophone Sub-Saharan Africa are a unique feature of the program. Since 1961 Kalamazoo has led in placing undergraduates in these institutions. A number of regular Africa-oriented courses are supplemented by an extensive summer cocurricular program of lectures, cultural events, and social programs.

The foreign study component generates enthusiasm for an international focus in other areas of the college. Building on fluency in a language, the International Commerce Program enables about 20 students annually to develop capabilities in economics and finance that are broadened by foreign travel and study of foreign politics, history, and sociology. The European Research Quarter enables four to six students to do their required Senior Individualized Project (SIP) during the spring quarter of their junior year (following a two-term foreign study program) in Freiburg, Germany and Colmar, France.

HOW ORGANIZED. The Foreign Study Program is administered by a director who reports to the president. With an associate, they maintain relationships with established foreign centers, make travel plans, orient students for foreign study, and visit them at the sites. The budget is $960,000 and is enhanced by an endowment. Costs to students are equivalent to those on campus. Students apply for sites in accordance with language facility and academic ability and interests. Actual placement is made by the foreign study director in consultation with other faculty. Whenever possible, students are fully integrated into foreign universities. In some cases they take special courses arranged for them. Course work is usually in language, literature, fine arts, and social studies, although qualified students may enroll in other disciplines. In the quarter prior to foreign study, students attend weekly required orientation sessions aimed at preparing them to study, live, and travel in foreign settings.

The European Research Quarter is directed by two faculty members. Enrollment must follow the foreign study quarter. Students are selected on the merit of proposed research topics and appropriateness for the foreign setting. The project is evaluated as any other Senior Individualized Project and receives two units of credit. Total cost is comparable to the SIP quarter if done away from campus within the U.S.

The International Commerce Program, directed by two faculty members, is open to students regardless of major. The concentration requires five economics courses, skill in a second language, and a social science elective that emphasizes international study. Additionally, the student must participate in the Foreign Study Program and complete an internationally focused Senior Individualized Project.

EDUCATIONAL IMPACT.   The Foreign Study Program is integral to the curriculum and to the K Plan. Encouraged by the success of an experimental Summer Foreign Study Program, the college arranged its present calendar to provide foreign study for virtually all students. The curriculum was organized so students could easily meet all requirements and still study abroad. Foreign study is seen as essential to educational development.

Because students have such an intensive foreign experience, many courses in political science, sociology and anthropology, economics, and art have been redesigned to include cross-cultural perspectives and an international focus. The International Commerce Program was developed to meet business world needs for graduates with language skills and knowledge of foreign cultures. Extracurricular programs began to include international dimensions because of changed student perspectives.

Foreign students are encouraged to attend Kalamazoo College as special students or degree candidates to enhance the cross-cultural infusion started by the Foreign Study Program. Kalamazoo College has extended its campus to include foreign settings and internationalized its curriculum in the hope that students will be better prepared to deal with concerns that cross national boundaries.

RESOURCE PERSON.   Joe Fugate, Director of Foreign Study, Kalamazoo College, Kalamazoo, MI 49007. Phone: (616) 383-8470.

LAFAYETTE COLLEGE, Easton, PA

Lafayette, founded by the citizens of Easton in 1826, is an independent, coeducational institution offering undergraduate degrees in the arts, sciences, and engineering. The college enrolls about 2,050, employs about 150 faculty (of which 85 percent hold doctoral degrees), and has an endowment of more than $60 million. Though most of Lafayette students are from New Jersey, Pennsylvania, and New York, 36 states and 19 foreign countries are represented. Over 70 percent of entering freshmen rank in the top 10 percent of their secondary school classes, and about 90 percent of seniors find full-time employment or begin advanced study shortly after graduation.

INTERNATIONAL ASPECTS OF THE CURRICULUM. *The International Affairs Program*, over 30 years old, is an interdisciplinary course of study designed for students who seek a broad awareness of world affairs and foreign policy, as well as those interested specifically in foreign service and international business. The program is built on the assumption that international relations requires the scholarly insights and analytical tools of several fields. While specializing in international affairs (IA) and obtaining a BA, the student acquires a broad liberal arts education.

The International Affairs Program is interdepartmental. To major in IA the student must complete a series of courses offered by four departments (economics, government and law, history, and languages), in addition to a year-long International Affairs senior seminar. Freshmen and sophomores intending to major in International Affairs continue or begin their language training on a level determined by the languages department. The IA language requirement is met by completing three years of language instruction; many IA majors take a fourth year or venture into a second or even a third language.

During their first two years at Lafayette prospective IA majors are encouraged to take a series of preparatory courses: Introduction to International Politics, Historical Background to the Contemporary World, Macro- and Micro-Economics. To meet the major's advanced requirements, the student takes 4 IA-related courses (out of 14) offered by the Department of Government and Law, four in the history department (out of 13), two in international economics (out of 4), and the senior seminar, which integrates the entire program. Seniors of high ability are encouraged to do an honors thesis under the guidance of a teacher.

The International Affairs Program is the most structured of all Lafayette's social science and humanities courses of study. It requires a maximum of 22 introductory and advanced courses (5 in government, 5 in history, 4 in economics, 6 in languages, 2 in international affairs). However, the breadth and diversity of the curricular requirements prevents parochialism.

HOW ORGANIZED. Lafayette's International Affairs Program is headed by a full-time faculty member who is also a member of one of the departments most directly involved in offering IA-related courses. The program's chairman is responsible directly to the provost and to the president. He chairs the IA Advisory Committee, manages the departmental budget, serves as advisor to IA majors, and assists in the activities of the International Relations (IR) Club.

The faculty IA Advisory Committee assists the chairman. Economics, government, history, and language departments are represented on the committee.

EDUCATIONAL IMPACT. IA majors and other Lafayette students have additional opportunities to expand their international awareness and knowledge. IA majors are encouraged to spend a year or a semester abroad; the majority go to France, Germany, or Spain. While Lafayette works in cooperation with a few American institutions specializing in such programs, the college has, in the last few years, developed its own interim program abroad, a series of three-credit interdisciplinary study trips offered in the six weeks between the fall and spring semesters. These have been organized in Austria, Cuba, England, France, Israel, and the People's Republic of China.

The academic program in International Affairs is also supplemented by a variety of extracurricular programs. Many of these are organized by the IR Club, which is managed by students, primarily IA majors. The club sponsors films, lectures, panels, and trips related to international affairs.

Recent IA graduates have pursued graduate work in international management, international studies, public administration, and law. They have been hired by accounting firms, major corporations, banks, advertising firms, and government agencies.

RESOURCE PERSON. Ilan Peleg, Department of Government, Lafayette College, Easton, PA 18042. Phone: (215) 253-6281, x319.

LEHIGH UNIVERSITY, Bethlehem, PA

Lehigh is a private coeducational university founded in 1865, with approximately 4,200 undergraduates and 2,000 graduate students. It includes the colleges of arts and science, business and economics, and engineering and physical sciences, which offer graduate and undergraduate degrees; the School of Education offers graduate programs only. Some 425 faculty, of whom 70 percent hold doctorates, teach 1,750 courses. The university's annual budget is over $55 million and it has an endowment of $54 million. Most students come from New Jersey, Pennsylvania, and New York. The 200-acre campus is 60 miles north of Philadelphia and 90 miles west of New York. Three quarters of Lehigh's alumni are currently employed by business and industry; Lehigh ranks fifth in the country in the proportion of its alumni who are officers or directors of their corporations.

INTERNATIONAL ASPECTS OF THE CURRICULUM. Lehigh offers majors in international relations, modern foreign languages, and foreign careers (an interdisciplinary program with a strong business and economics component coupled with foreign language and culture) as well as minors in these fields and in Latin-American and Russian studies. International relations majors are strongly encouraged to study a language and to spend at least one semester abroad in an accredited academic program. The 50 students are given a broad foundation in the basic elements of the international system along with a regional or functional emphasis designed to meet the needs of each. The number of majors has risen steadily over the last decade, as have overall enrollments in the 40 courses offered by the department—which were taken by 1,250 students in 1980-81. The Department of Modern Foreign Languages has increased its course offerings to include society and culture and has recently begun to teach Hebrew, Portuguese, and Chinese. The department has 21 majors and 37 minors, foreign careers has 15 majors, Latin-American studies has 8 minors, and international relations has 41 minors.

HOW ORGANIZED. The international relations department has been autonomous within the College of Arts and Science for three decades. With six full-time faculty and a number of adjuncts, it is one of the largest of its type in the country. Almost all of its $180,000 budget is provided by the university. The department's operations are monitored by the annual Visiting Committee, composed of senior officials in government departments and major corporations and leading academics from major universities. In addition, alumni are encouraged to visit the department, give lectures or seminars, and provide career guidance for international relations majors.

Lehigh is developing an academic exchange program with a number of British universities and has for many years sent students abroad in programs run by other colleges and universities. These programs are approved by the departments in which the students major. Many students also serve internationally oriented internships with government departments, corporations, and nonprofit organizations; often these are combined with independent study or directed reading for academic credit.

Courses offered by five other colleges in the Lehigh Valley are open to Lehigh students through a cross-registration procedure operated by the Lehigh Valley

Association of Independent Colleges. There is a limited program of faculty exchange to improve the range of course offerings in certain areas, such as African and Latin-American studies.

EDUCATIONAL IMPACT. The high enrollment in international relations courses can be attributed to the longevity and size of the department as well as to the range and quality of offerings and the growing interest in global education. Since many Lehigh students are business oriented, the realities of global economic interdependence have rendered international relations courses useful to them. Over the last decade courses have shifted from a traditional historical "great power" approach toward a more diverse systemic and functional one, covering such subjects as international technology transfer and the competition for natural resources.

The international relations department has collaborated with the technical and engineering departments to provide an international dimension. In addition, the department has participated in externally funded projects to inject a global perspective into technical and social studies education at the secondary and post-secondary levels. The most recent is a series of workshops for 60 social studies teachers from area high schools on the global dimensions of the energy crisis.

International affairs enters campus life through the International Relations Club, which has the largest membership of any special-interest student organization and sponsors speakers, ethnic dinners, foreign films, and debates each semester. A German House and an International House provide alternative living arrangements for both American and international students and there are regular meal tables for those speaking French, Spanish, and Italian. Lehigh sends delegations to the National, Harvard, and Princeton Model UN sessions and the international relations department gives credit for this work. The Commons Room of the department, which offers foreign newspapers and periodicals, has become an informal gathering place for students and faculty interested in international affairs, thus helping to dispel any impression that a global perspective is the exclusive preserve of the department.

RESOURCE PERSON. Michael Hodges, Chairman, Department of International Relations, Lehigh University, Bethlehem, PA 18015. Phone: (215) 861-3390.

LEWIS AND CLARK COLLEGE, Portland, OR

Lewis and Clark College is a four-year independent liberal arts institution founded by Presbyterian pioneers in Albany, Oregon in 1867 and moved to Portland in 1942. The college offers BA and BS degrees and enrolls 1,800; in addition, 700 students are studying for the master's and 600 are enrolled in the law school. There are 115 full-time undergraduate and 56 part-time undergraduate faculty, of which 92 percent hold the highest degrees appropriate to their disciplines. The college's budget in 1979 was $16.5 million.

INTERNATIONAL ASPECTS OF THE CURRICULUM. Lewis and Clark has interrelated programs that provide the campus with an intercultural environment. All freshmen take a one-year program called Society and Culture that includes ten courses, each considering some aspect of the history of human culture. Six contain a good deal of non-Western material and have an explicit intercultural comparative purpose. Within three years all courses in the program will be intercultural and comparative. The program's aim is to introduce students to the college curriculum while emphasizing that the material is global and not confined to the Western tradition.

For 17 years Lewis and Clark has had an overseas study program. Each year 5 or 6 groups of approximately 25, normally led by a Lewis and Clark faculty member, study a culture abroad for two quarters. The college also sends smaller groups each year to particular locations for special programs; for example, the winter or summer term is spent in Costa Rica for Spanish training. There is a Junior Year Abroad program at the University of Munich for a full academic year; students from Reed College and Willamette University also participate. A singular feature of the Lewis and Clark overseas study program is the change of study locations each year. Except for special programs like those in Costa Rica and Munich, the college maintains no programs in permanent locations. Another feature is study groups in Asia, Africa, Latin America, and eastern Europe. In 1982 the college will send its first study group to the Republic of China in an exchange with a Chinese university. Each program is tailored to the country in question. The overseas study program is part of the college's general education curriculum; it is not attached to a particular department or division. Students in all years are encouraged to apply.

In addition to the conversational training students receive abroad, there is a language program on campus, with majors in French, Spanish, and German and courses in Japanese, Italian, Greek, Latin, and Russian. The international affairs curriculum at Lewis and Clark is a recognized interdisciplinary major with over 100 students each year. A high percentage continue in graduate international studies programs. The Institute for the Study of American Language and Culture brings over 100 non-English-speaking students each year to campus so they can study English in an experiential education curriculum tailored to their needs.

HOW ORGANIZED. The freshman Society and Culture program is directed by an associate dean of faculty on a half-time basis. The director works with a general studies subcommittee of the Curriculum Committee. There is a small budget to reimburse departments for teaching time and to pay for teaching materials in the 10 courses. Society and Culture faculty are drawn from all departments, with a majority from the humanities. In January 1980 the college received a three-year grant from the National Endowment for the Humanities to assist in the development of new courses. In each of three summers regular faculty attend a month-long seminar on materials to be incorporated into Society and Culture courses. In summer 1980 the seminar was on East Asia.

The overseas study program is headed by an associate dean of faculty and director whose full-time responsibility includes the overseas program, the Institute for the Study of American Language and Culture, and the foreign students on campus. The director works with an overseas study subcommittee of the Curriculum Committee. Students studying overseas pay a comprehensive fee that exceeds the cost of on-campus room, board, tuition, and incidentals by about $200. Air transportation and all student costs from departure to return are borne by the college. The cost of replacing overseas faculty leaders is charged to the overseas study program.

Foreign languages and literatures and international affairs are regular academic departments.

EDUCATIONAL IMPACT. The Society and Culture program, with its comparative cultural emphasis, is new to the college. It builds on the 17-year experience with overseas study. About half of the students who graduate each spring have spent at least two terms overseas. A few go more than once. When the design of the Society and Culture program is fully realized, all students will have had one year of comparative study and may then go on to study abroad or to major in languages, international affairs, or some other discipline incorporating materials from the whole world culture.

The college's aim in developing these programs has been to infuse the entire curriculum with an international outlook. Graduates are intended to have a global awareness appropriate to a culturally interdependent world.

RESOURCE PERSON. David W. Savage, Lewis and Clark College, 0615 S.W. Palatine Hill Road, Portland, OR 97219. Phone: (503) 244-6161, x351.

LOCK HAVEN STATE COLLEGE, Lock Haven, PA

Lock Haven State College is a multipurpose institution offering the BA and BS in arts and science, the BS in education, and the BS in health, physical education, and recreation. It is coeducational, with an enrollment of 2,500 students, most residential. The college has a strong undergraduate program, offers no graduate credit, and is one of the 14 state-owned institutions of higher education in Pennsylvania. It has 163 full-time and 3 part-time faculty, of which approximately 56 percent hold doctorates. The total operating budget is $13.9 million.

INTERNATIONAL ASPECTS OF THE CURRICULUM. Lock Haven State offers a Bachelor of Arts with a major in international studies, designed to provide an interdisciplinary perspective for examining the world community. The objective is to educate the student who seeks a career in international business, government, education, or law or who wants graduate study in international affairs. Up to 12 semester hours in a language, 2 world history courses, and world regional geography are required of these majors.

Lock Haven students may study abroad in exchange programs with the Nottingham College of Education, Marie Curie Sklodowska University in Lublin, Poland, or Kelvin Grove College of Education in Brisbane, Australia. In addition, students may do part of their student teaching in the American Schools in Quito, Ecuador and those in several countries in Western Europe. Faculty also participate in these exchanges. More than 550 American and foreign students and about 50 faculty have taken part since the first program began in 1971. The college is also a member of the Pennsylvania Consortium for International Education, which operates summer schools in Salzburg, Austria and in Mexico.

A full-time director supervises these programs. He is assisted by several faculty who serve as coordinators. A special budget is available for managing the programs and additional funds come from the U.S. State Department. Reduced air fares have been arranged through the embassies of these countries to lower costs to students and faculty.

The college also administers an exchange in which about 70 master teachers from the Province of Buenos Aires, Argentina spend a semester in an American college or university studying the American school system. This program is co-sponsored by the American Association of State Colleges and Universities. Faculty from the host institutions are sent to Argentina for up to a semester.

Foreign exchange students and faculty take part in classroom discussions, seminars, a lecture series, the International Club, and the Model UN each spring. These exchange participants help prepare new groups en route to another country; they explain the cultural heritage of the country and its people, and help in acquiring modest language skills where needed.

HOW ORGANIZED. Anyone in good academic standing in any degree program may apply for a student exchange. Course selection is aided by faculty advisors and is supervised on site by the accompanying Lock Haven faculty. A professor travels to each American school where a student is teaching once a semester to evaluate the school and the student's work. Most cost is defrayed by a special fee charged to each student assigned to an overseas school. Students on exchange pay room, board, and tuition to Lock Haven State and simply exchange beds with their counterparts from the other countries. Credits earned are transferred to Lock Haven. Evaluation of course equivalency is done before the program is implemented.

Faculty exchanges are negotiated directly between faculty. Entire homes are involved and local currency is deposited in a bank for the use of the visitors so that no money flows from the country. Faculty travel broadly on these exchanges at their own expense. An orientation is provided for those planning exchanges and they are debriefed on their return. Participating faculty become resource people for the Office of International Education, for other faculty in their classrooms, and for an OIE-sponsored lecture series.

EDUCATIONAL IMPACT. Students describe their lives as dramatically changed as a result of participating in these exchanges, particularly those who have spent a semester in a socialist country. As most are from rural communities, the experience provides an international dimension they could not acquire solely from the classroom. Students and faculty become much less parochial in their outlook on national and international affairs. Some graduates who participated as student teachers return for full-time employment in the host country.

The international education program is accepted enthusiastically by both faculty and students. The Pennsylvania state department of education has recognized the college's achievements in this area. Value can be measured in terms of widened global perspectives of students and faculty from Pennsylvania and several other states who have participated.

RESOURCE PERSON. Jorge Mottet, Director, Office of International Education, Lock Haven State College, Lock Haven, PA 17745. Phone: (717) 893-2140.

MACALESTER COLLEGE, St. Paul, MN

Macalester was founded in 1885 as a privately supported four-year liberal arts college. While affiliated with the United Presbyterian Church, the college is nonsectarian in its instruction and attitudes. Macalester enrolls 1,728 undergraduates and has a diverse student body. Over 50 percent come from outside Minnesota, 8 percent are minority, and 8 percent are foreign students from 41 nations. The college has 125 full-time and 34 part-time faculty and 85 percent have doctorates. It has an annual budget of $14 million and an endowment of $21 million. Macalester offers the BA in 34 major fields, with special programs in pre-engineering, nursing, Latin-American studies, premedicine, and prelaw. Since 1971 Macalester students have been awarded 27 Fulbright-Hayes scholarships, 5 Danforth fellowships, and 3 Rhodes scholarships.

INTERNATIONAL ASPECTS OF THE CURRICULUM. The Macalester *International Studies Program* has three major components: curricular, experiential, and skills development. Participants major in anthropology, French, German/Russian, economics, geography, history, philosophy, political science, religious studies, or Spanish. In addition, students must complete at least six additional courses outside their major but within the participating departments that support their primary interest. Students are urged to include at least two interdisciplinary topical seminars of global or intercultural concern. The participation of the World Press Institute and foreign students in these seminars is encouraged. Each International Studies major must spend at least one semester on a study-abroad program or at a foreign university. Majors must demonstrate competence in at least one foreign language, oral and written communication in English, and bibliographic skills. The program attracts approximately 25 majors a year.

Many other units at the college offer programs that support Macalester's international emphasis. Each year the Hubert Humphrey and Mitau lecture series brings a number of distinguished speakers on international affairs. The International Center sponsors a wide variety of programs, including workshops on foreign student adjustment, intercultural communications, films, and faculty-led International Forums. The World Press Institute brings 12 journalists from around the world to the campus each fall. The French, German, Spanish, and Russian houses permit students to practice their language skills with fellow students and with the native speakers in residence. More than 50 percent of Macalester students participate in study-abroad programs. Approximately 75 percent of those take part in the 18 programs designated as especially appropriate to Macalester's curriculum. Each January one Macalester professor receives a faculty stipend to do research abroad in order to develop a new course with international content. Three campus publications are devoted to international issues: the Macalester International Journal, the Focal Point, and the Tartan International, a newsletter sent to Macalester students abroad.

HOW ORGANIZED. Macalester's International Studies Program, under the supervision of the vice president for academic affairs, has a coordinator and an advisory committee composed of five representatives from the participating departments. Funding for the program comes from the regular budgets of the affiliated departments.

In order to foster an integrated and coordinated approach to international education on a campuswide basis, the coordinator of the International Studies Program and the director of the International Center serve on the Macalester International Programs Committee. In spring 1980 the academic vice president chaired a workshop to make recommendations on the future of international education at the college. The International Center has an annual budget of approximately $110,000. In addition, the International Center awards $33,000 in supplemental grants to enable students to study abroad. Returnees complete evaluation forms to help assess the quality and appropriateness of the programs. In 1979 and 1980 foreign students completed questionnaires evaluating their experiences at the college.

Macalester views the International Studies Program study abroad and the foreign student program as integral and highly significant components of its curriculum. These and other international programs are seen as crucial in supporting and maintaining the college's international emphasis.

EDUCATIONAL IMPACT. According to the admissions department, a large number of students select Macalester because of its international programs. Approximately 50 percent of freshmen have already had an international experience; at graduation more than three fourths of the student body has been abroad. The large percentage of courses with an international component helps prepare students for study abroad and provides fruitful ways for returnees to take advantage of their experiences. The presence of over 150 foreign students allows Macalester students to experience much of the world on their home campus. Foreign students contribute valuable information and new perspectives in the classroom and, less formally, in dormitories, dining commons, and in casual social situations. In the most recent Long-Range Plan, the college has reaffirmed its commitment to international education and has designated it as one of the areas in which Macalester excels.

RESOURCE PERSON. David B. Sanford, Director, International Center, Macalester College, St. Paul, MN 55105. Phone: (612) 647-6310.

MICHIGAN STATE UNIVERSITY, East Lansing, MI

Founded in 1855, Michigan State (MSU) was the first U.S. agricultural land-grant college. It has nearly 200 undergraduate programs and 76 areas for graduate students, taught by more than 3,000 faculty in 16 colleges and the Graduate School. Fall 1979 enrollment was 44,756—36,372 undergraduates, 7,150 graduates, and 1,234 professional students. About 85 percent are Michigan residents; among the remainder are more than 1,300 international students from 95 countries. MSU operates on the quarter system. The general education program requires a learning core apart from specialized disciplines, and Madison and Briggs colleges provide a small-college setting. MSU offers lifelong education programs, the Cooperative Extension Service, a research program of more than 3,000 projects, and the Office of International Studies and Programs.

INTERNATIONAL ASPECTS OF THE CURRICULUM. The undergraduate programs in international education are, by design, decentralized. Courses on non-Western cultural traditions are an integral part of the general education sequence. Languages are offered in two departments and innovative approaches are followed for those not commonly taught. Study-abroad programs provide overseas experiences for about 700 students each year. One residential college, James Madison, offers an international relations concentration and has an active Model UN group.

In the College of Social Science, the undergraduate Multidisciplinary Program, with about 800 majors, has an international relations/global studies track. Each of seven area studies provides an undergraduate certificate program. Three of these also plan, coordinate, and monitor area courses in the university's interdisciplinary course curriculum. Two departments—history and anthropology—have produced a special combined sequence of courses in global studies. This joint effort has been coordinated with the College of Education's Global Studies Center, whose personnel have been assisting in the development of international education in the Michigan school system.

MSU faculty have been extensively involved in overseas development projects; their departments offer courses that treat world health, food, energy, and other global issues. In all MSU offers more than 400 courses that deal with international education.

HOW ORGANIZED. Created in 1956, the Office of the Dean of International Studies and Programs (ISP) is mainly responsible for adding and coordinating the international dimension throughout the university. It is active in technical assistance and development research projects with scholars in developing countries around the world. It is also concerned with graduate and undergraduate international education. The dean has direct access to the university provost. Overseas development projects are financed by external sponsors, while international studies activities are part of the regular budget. Study abroad is supported by student fees.

Because studies of a comparative, international, or global orientation are given throughout the university, ISP does not offer courses or degrees. The evaluation of international courses is accomplished internally by the academic units concerned. ISP does, however, aid communication among faculty about international affairs by means of activities sponsored by ISP area studies units, international institutes, and an informal faculty network known as the Global Issues Group.

EDUCATIONAL IMPACT. MSU strives to have the many components of international studies and programs reinforce each other. Overseas projects provide feedback to campus programs; study abroad relates to area studies; area specialists consult with technical project personnel; international student programs concern area studies and cocurricular efforts; and so on. The Office of International Studies and Programs, at the center of these, has thus been directly involved with goals and strategy for the entire university—seeking and managing resources, bringing departments and other units together, keeping abreast of new opportunities, strengthening faculty competence in an international direction. The office shares responsibility with units in all parts of the university and its impact—weak or strong—is diffused throughout. At the same time, this diffusion approach is what makes MSU's international dimensions effective.

RESOURCE PERSON. Ralph H. Smuckler, Dean, International Studies and Programs, Michigan State University, East Lansing, MI 48824. Phone: (517) 355-2352.

MIDDLEBURY COLLEGE, Middlebury, VT

Middlebury was founded in 1800 at the behest of the local citizenry, who provided most of the financing. In 1883 women were admitted, making the college one of the earliest coeducational institutions of its type. Its summer language programs go back to the foundation of the German School in 1915, and since then French, Italian, Russian, Spanish, Chinese, and Japanese have been added; there is also a graduate school of English and an annual Writers' Conference on the Bread Loaf Mountain campus. Middlebury's 1,900 undergraduates are taught in the regular session by a faculty of about 140. There are 1,400 graduates and undergraduates in the summer language schools, and the faculty, drawn largely from other institutions, also numbers about 140.

INTERNATIONAL ASPECTS OF THE CURRICULUM. While many aspects of the regular academic program are devoted to international studies—such as courses in language and literature, history, political science, economics, and the like—a most unusual feature is the summer language program. Most participants are pursuing undergraduate or graduate degrees at Middlebury or other institutions, but a number also come from business, commerce, international law, and the government.

The *five schools of Western languages* offer, besides introductory language training at the undergraduate level, two graduate degree programs leading toward the MA and the doctorate of modern languages. Only the Chinese and Japanese schools offer no advanced degrees, and their students come mainly from other colleges and universities, as well as from the community. There are, in addition, a variety of ways regular Middlebury undergraduates are encouraged to take language training during the summer intensive sessions, as well as at the schools overseas. Language departments work closely with other departments and divisions of the college to encourage students majoring in other scientific or humanistic disciplines to achieve proficiency in a foreign language in their chosen fields. Indeed, the schools' earlier emphasis on literature and literary criticism has, in the last several years, been making way for an increasing concern with the culture, history, economics, and politics of the countries being studied. Earning one of the advanced degrees at Middlebury normally means not only work in the college's summer program, but study abroad at one of the five Middlebury schools overseas, in Florence, Madrid, Mainz, Moscow, or Paris.

HOW ORGANIZED. The summer language schools insist that all work and daily communication be conducted in the schools' individual languages. A partial exception is made for beginners; otherwise students sign pledges to use no English during the summer sessions. They live in dormitories with other students and faculty of their school, dine with them, and participate in the extracurricular activities arranged by the school. The aim is total immersion, so that the student gradually becomes accustomed not only to writing and speaking, but to thinking, in the language he or she is learning.

The language schools, both abroad and at Middlebury, are directed by the vice president for foreign languages. The directors of the individual schools (most from faculties of other institutions) and the directors of studies of the schools abroad (most from the regular Middlebury faculty) report to him. The directors of the language schools are responsible for hiring their own faculties each summer;

since there are no tenured faculty, the schools can make innovations promptly to meet changing student needs. The total combined budget for the summer intensive session and the schools abroad was about $2.5 million for 1978-79.

EDUCATIONAL IMPACT.   Middlebury's commitment to international education has long been reflected by its language schools; despite the discrete nature of the summer sessions and the schools abroad, it has worked hard to keep all these as part of a single college. Thus the vice president for foreign languages works closely with the other academic officers to coordinate the offerings of the language programs with those of the regular academic year and to ensure that the strengths of the different sessions complement one another. Hence not only the language and literature departments, but other international and area studies programs (such as East Asian Studies) profit from the presence of the language schools. This cooperation has grown measurably in the last few years as the national emphasis on international studies increases.

RESOURCE PERSON.   Nicholas R. Clifford, Vice President for Academic Affairs, Old Chapel, Middlebury College, Middlebury, VT 05753. Phone: (802) 388-7963.

MIDDLESEX COUNTY COLLEGE, Edison, NJ

Middlesex County College, a comprehensive community college, admitted its first class in September 1966. Enrollment has increased from 728 full-time and 800 part-time students to 5,000 full-time, 7,000 part-time, and over 18,000 community education students in 1979-80. More than 550 credit and 800 noncredit courses are offered, including cooperative work experiences, clinical involvement, work-study programs overseas, and laboratory assignments that parallel classroom studies. Its 23 satellite centers supplement the main 250-acre campus, which has 28 buildings valued at over $55,000,000. It has 215 full-time and 79 adjunct instructors.

INTERNATIONAL ASPECTS OF THE CURRICULUM. The goal of the international education program is to add an international dimension to existing programs and departments through cultural activities, curriculum revisions, staff development in-service seminars and courses, new course offerings, special business-oriented educational endeavors, and the building of an international studies library collection. A team of 25 faculty representing different disciplines have participated in the staff development program, implementing curricular changes and developing new courses on campus and abroad. Participating faculty have attended curriculum retreats and have followed in-house, custom-designed graduate courses on international education. The college has meetings for faculty with international speakers. Teachers have prepared such monographs as International Component in Nurse Education, The International Dimension of Teaching Economics, World Environmental Concerns in the Classroom, Integrating Global Perspectives Into a College Reading Improvement Course, and International Dimensions in the Teaching of Mathematics, Chisanbop.

Middlesex offers courses toward a 21-credit certificate program in international business. It includes three general business courses—Business Organization and Management, Marketing I, and General Economics; three international business courses—Introduction to International Business, International Marketing, and International Transportation and Distribution; and Comparative Political and Cultural Systems, which is designed to give business students a cross-cultural understanding. For the certificate program in export documentation students must complete Introduction to Trade, International Letters of Credit, Exporting Techniques and Documentation, and International Transportation.

One community-based program is the Middlesex International Round Table. Local people involved in international commerce participate in a business discussion group that meets monthly to exchange views on world trade and to hear guest speakers. There are also conferences for the business community, planned by the Office of International Studies and offered through the Division of Community Education, on such topics as How to Do International Market Research, What Every Business Person Should Know About International Banking, and Shipping Hazardous Materials.

An extensive study-abroad program is being developed in England, Spain, and Israel. In Spain American students work as language tutors to Spanish children during the summer in exchange for room and board. The English program is theater and literature oriented, while the Israeli program is in the technologies.

HOW ORGANIZED. Middlesex's program is headed by a director who reports to the vice president of the college. He devotes half time to this program and su pervises bilingual programs, English as a second language courses, and foreigr students. There are also an International Education Committee and a Bilingual Education Committee. A community advisory group representing county businesses advises the program director and serves as a resource for faculty and students. The International Education Committee is divided into five subcommittees: travel programs, staff development, curriculum, foreign students, and cultural activities. The program started with state and federal funding but tuition revenues have made it self-sustaining. The program director consults with the seven divisional deans on programs affecting their areas.

EDUCATIONAL IMPACT. The international project, with a mailing list containing nearly 8,000 potential exporters, has enabled the college to reach a new constituency. The project has brought in substantial sums in funding, tuition, fees, and FTEs. It has added a new collection of international education and international business titles to the library. It has brought together administrators and faculty from diverse disciplines to examine their assumptions about global education and to improve the curriculum. Its impact has been widespread: The modern languages department is discussing a new cooperative study-travel program to Spain, the engineering department is preparing a course integrating global elements, and the business department is considering a major in international business.

RESOURCE PERSON. Virgil H. Blanco, Office of the Vice President, Academic Services Building, Middlesex County College, Edison, NJ 08818. Phone: (201) 548-6000, x281.

MONROE COMMUNITY COLLEGE, Rochester, NY

Established in 1961 by the county of Monroe as part of the State University of New York, Monroe Community College is a comprehensive, two-year institution serving more than 10,000 full- and part-time students. Located in the city of Rochester, it serves an area with a vigorous economy marked by high technology, multinational corporations, and international trade. The student body reflects the racial and ethnic diversity of the county's half million people. Monroe offers a variety of associate degree programs and special educational services to meet the community's diverse needs. Degree programs consist of both university parallel curricula and occupation-centered courses of study. Emphases include liberal arts and sciences, business, health sciences, public service, and engineering technologies. About 30 percent of students register in transfer curricula, with 70 percent in career programs. General education courses are required of students in all curricula.

INTERNATIONAL ASPECTS OF THE CURRICULUM. Monroe's international education program has two interrelated dimensions: programs relating to the credit-bearing curriculum and noncredit, community service programs. The general objective in the curriculum is to develop the capabilities of faculty and students to comprehend and function effectively in an interdependent and culturally diverse world. This is achieved through carefully organized, institutionally pervasive programs of faculty development, which to date have involved about one third of the faculty; curricular revisions to enhance the international dimensions of general education through the incorporation of international, global, and cross-cultural concerns in numerous courses in the humanities and social and natural sciences; further development of language and international components in selected degree programs in liberal arts, business, and engineering technologies; opportunities for overseas study, some emphasizing international business; and cocurricular activities that strengthen the college community's receptivity to international concerns and provide support for the curricular emphases. These dimensions provide basic competence in world affairs and enhance the employability of graduates in internationally oriented occupations in the local economy, throughout the nation, and abroad.

In programs directed to the community the college provides opportunities for public education on international issues through forums that are sponsored in cooperation with the Rochester Association for the United Nations; the League of Women Voters; the World Trade Council of the Chamber of Commerce; county political committees; and church, labor, and civic groups. Monroe also organizes special conferences and seminars concerned with such topics as Eurocommunism, the economics of international migrant labor, and Middle East problems. It conducts programs in cooperation with ethnic groups—for example, a Black Cultural Heritage Program and educational activities with the local Bureau of Jewish Education and the Puerto Rican Arts and Cultural Center. The college offers special services to enhance the capabilities of local businesses to function in the international market, such as a conference on international trade and education in cooperation with the New York State Board of Regents and a seminar on American Business, the U.S. Government, and Africa's Development in the 80s.

HOW ORGANIZED. International education at Monroe is administered by the coordinator of international/intercultural programs, who reports to the vice president of academic affairs. Curricular revisions are facilitated by the coordinator in consultation with academic departments. Innovations in curricula are generally effected through faculty development projects emphasizing interdisciplinary study of international and cultural issues. The coordinator also works through the academic governance organization and its various committees to advance policies supportive of international education. Student support is achieved through special workshops for student government leaders. The college curriculum is coordinated with programs at four-year institutions to enhance transfer opportunities. Cooperative arrangements exist with consortia such as the Rochester Area College, the International/Intercultural Consortium of the American Association of Community and Junior Colleges, and the College Consortium on International Studies.

The college's community outreach is implemented in close cooperation with sectors of the community cited above. In organizing programs Monroe makes available to local business and civic groups the resources of federal and state agencies, such as the U.S. Department of State, and national and district offices of the U.S. Department of Commerce.

Institutional resources and special funding provide financial support for international education. The college funds the coordinator's position and some activities. Special programs have been financed by grants received locally and from the New York Council on the Humanities, the U.S. Department of Education, and the National Endowment for the Humanities. The latter have been critical for the curricular reform programs.

EDUCATIONAL IMPACT. The international education program has heightened faculty, staff, and student sensitivities to the far-reaching changes in the international environment and has established foundations for appreciation of cultural diversity. Interdisciplinary approaches in curriculum reform have brought together faculty from several disciplines in addressing global concerns. Individual faculty are now assuming responsibility for their own professional development outside the college. Students are increasingly taking leadership in organizing programs through their associations, including formulation of policy and allocation of funds for programs concerned with local-global links. Community-oriented programs have gained the confidence of area organizations and corporations, which are increasingly coming to see Monroe as the appropriate place for responsible and informed discussions of international affairs and as a source of assistance in employee training. These community relationships have benefited the college's more traditional academic programs and students, promoting dialogue between campus and community on the significant global questions of our times.

RESOURCE PERSON. Sumati Devadutt, Coordinator of International/Intercultural Programs, Monroe Community College, Rochester, NY 14623. Phone: (716) 424-5200.

MT. HOOD COMMUNITY COLLEGE, Gresham, OR

Mt. Hood Community College was founded in 1965 and opened in 1966. The college district (950 square miles, with a population of 200,000) is next to Portland and encompasses suburban, rural, and industrial areas. The college offers 65 pre-professional lower-division programs and 60 vocational programs. Occupational upgrading is also a concern and many needing retraining do this at Mt. Hood. Approximately 3,200 full-time and 6,800 part-time students are enrolled, a full-time equivalent of about 6,000. The average student age is 29. A full-time faculty of 163, 550 part-time faculty, and 39 administrators serve the college, which is governed by a board of 5 elected citizens.

INTERNATIONAL ASPECTS OF THE CURRICULUM. The international education program has several components. Study-abroad programs that usually include an experiential or occupational component have operated for a decade. For example, automotive students visited automobile factories in Germany, nursing students studied health care in Nepal, and early childhood education majors participated in child care in England and Scandinavia.

A two-year lower-division program in international studies is offered, from which students may transfer to the state colleges and universities. Participants pursue an area of concentration (Latin America, Asia, or Europe) and take two years of an appropriate language, two terms of introductory international studies, and three terms of a series called Contemporary Culture: The Global Village.

A two-year vocational program in international business starts in 1981. This includes one year of language and a year of either history of Eastern civilization or Western civilization, plus international marketing and international finance. Two other vocational programs (early childhood education and journalism) now include optional concentrations in international education.

Mt. Hood participates actively in the Pacific Northwest International/Intercultural Education Consortium and the coordinator of international education at Mt. Hood is a director for PNIIEC. Its purpose is to foster cooperation in study-abroad activities; share ideas, materials, and resources; and facilitate curriculum development and outreach.

There are 27 international students from 13 countries at Mt. Hood; Nigerians and Iranians form the majority. A special counselor is assigned to advise these students.

HOW ORGANIZED. The international education program is under the direction of a coordinator who reports directly to the dean of development. The coordinator's salary at present is paid one third by U.S. Department of Education grant funds and two thirds by the college budget.

Grants have mainly been used to develop instructional modules that can be integrated into existing courses. For example, a module on advertising techniques in foreign countries is a part of some business courses and one on transcultural communication is used in speech courses. The college has added these elements to popular courses in order to reach the greatest number of students. If materials were limited to special courses for international education majors, only a few students would be exposed to the richness of transcultural dimensions. About 40 instructional modules have been created by 25 faculty.

Teachers developing the modules are divided into three task forces, each representing an area—Latin America, Europe, Asia. Before a module is accepted for payment or release time, it must undergo peer review and be approved by the task force. The coordinator for international education and the dean for development give final approval.

Two standing committees also influence the international education program. A committee with representatives from all segments of the campus plus community members reviews all study-abroad programs. The President's Task Force, chaired by the dean of development, meets once a quarter to review all facets of the international education program and make plans.

EDUCATIONAL IMPACT. Mt Hood's commitment to international education led to an $82,000 U.S. Department of Education grant to develop a wider international curriculum. The direct result was the lower-division international studies program. The grant also made possible the sponsoring of monthly community forums held in conjunction with the Greater Gresham Chamber of Commerce. These feature nationally recognized leaders, often presented in cooperation with the local World Affairs Council. The forums are increasingly popular, with average attendance about 100. Participants have included not only those from the business and college communities but senior citizens and advanced high school students.

Mt. Hood's international education activities are publicized for students, staff, and faculty. This had led to greater faculty interest in travel and study abroad. A Group Study Abroad grant is expected to send 15 faculty to Taiwan and Hong Kong for 6 weeks in summer 1981. Each will conduct a research project and upon return will develop an instructional module for use at Mt. Hood. The modules will also be shared with the district's elementary and high schools. Also, academic year faculty exchanges are increasing.

A Research Office evaluation shows most students believe their courses were improved by the inclusion of international dimensions. In September 1981 an outside evaluator will review the entire international education program.

RESOURCE PERSON. Betty J. Pritchett, Dean of Development, or Mathilda Harris, Coordinator of International Education, Mt. Hood Community College, 26000 S.E. Stark, Gresham, OR 97030. Phone: (503) 667-7305.

OCCIDENTAL COLLEGE, Los Angeles, CA

Occidental is a coeducational liberal arts college founded in 1887 and located on 120 acres in a residential section of northeast Los Angeles. Its 1,600 students, two thirds of whom live on the campus, come from 40 states and 31 countries. There is a faculty of 114, supplemented by 20 part-time and adjunct professors. Occidental offers majors leading to the BA in 25 departments or areas. Independent study is emphasized in all courses and students may develop their own degree programs outside a conventional major. Campus facilities include 33 buildings and the library has 340,000 catalogued volumes. Over half the graduates go on to graduate or professional school.

INTERNATIONAL ASPECTS OF THE CURRICULUM. Among Occidental's primary aims are to help students appreciate the richness and diversity of cultural heritages, to prepare them for careers in international business or government service, and to increase international understanding as a basis for thoughtful citizenship. While many elements of the college serve these purposes, three international programs are described here.

The college maintains formal, year-long international study programs in five countries (England, France, Germany, Japan, and Spain), with about 50 students, selected competitively, participating each year. In addition, up to 10 students yearly may receive fellowships for independent research or creative work anywhere outside the United States.

Occidental offers three emphases in area studies—Asian, Hispanic/Latin-American, and Soviet—as well as minors in East Asian studies and a number of other regional studies. Each involves a multidisciplinary approach and covers the history, politics, economics, international relations, and culture of the area. The goal is to provide a broad background in the study of an area and to facilitate advanced research and independent study on topics of individual interest.

An interdisciplinary major in Diplomacy and World Affairs (DWA) prepares students for a wide spectrum of careers. The focus is on the modern period in the social sciences, and faculty from at least six departments teach in the program, which is supervised by its advisory committee. DWA students have participated for many years in the regional Model UN conferences, and a DWA Day is held each year on campus for outstanding students from the area. A large number of Occidental graduates enter the U.S. Foreign Service and many alumni hold senior diplomatic positions around the world.

HOW ORGANIZED. Other elements of Occidental's emphasis on international and cultural understanding include team-taught interdisciplinary courses in the core program on European, Latin-American, Asian, and Russian culture. Four such courses are required for graduation and these are usually taken in the freshman and sophomore years.

The college has a foreign language requirement for graduation. Chinese, French, German, Japanese, Russian, and Spanish are available. All teachers of required language courses are trained in the literature and culture of their languages; they include these components in their introductory courses and offer advanced courses for language majors and other qualified students. Some departments require or strongly recommend a language as part of the major.

The Faculty Committee on Educational Policy and Curriculum, which includes students as full voting members, oversees all aspects of the college's instructional program and periodically evaluates goals. In addition, there are faculty committees, also with student members, for international studies, multicultural education, area studies, and the Diplomacy and World Affairs program. Funding for these programs and activities comes from the regular budget, although the college occasionally receives grants for specific projects in the international field.

EDUCATIONAL IMPACT. In varying ways all students become involved from the freshman year onward in international education and well over half the faculty teach courses that further this commitment. The relatively large number of international students attending Occidental and living on campus contributes substantially in other ways. Clubs and organizations sponsor activities that offer additional opportunities for students and faculty.

RESOURCE PERSON. Dean of the Faculty, Occidental College, 1600 Campus Road, Los Angeles, CA 90041. Phone: (213) 259-2634.

THE OHIO STATE UNIVERSITY, Columbus, OH

Ohio State (OSU) is a land-grant university established in 1870. Total enrollment on all campuses for fall 1979 was 57,938, of whom 53,278 were on the Columbus campus. There were 44,961 undergraduates on all the campuses, mostly from Ohio. Some 47,150 of the Columbus campus students were from Ohio and 18,342 were from Franklin County, where the university is located. The 17 colleges offered 6,900 courses in 1978-79, with 181 undergraduate major programs and 108 graduate fields. Each year the university awards more than 10,000 degrees. For 1978 the university had 3,784 FTE instructional staff, for a faculty-student ratio of 20 to 1. The budget exceeds $500 million; about $20 million comes from endowment income and gifts and grants.

INTERNATIONAL ASPECTS OF THE CURRICULUM. Ohio State has an array of undergraduate programs with international dimensions. The core is centered in the College of Humanities and the College of Social and Behavioral Sciences, but virtually all the undergraduate colleges (including the professional ones, such as journalism and administrative science) have courses with global dimensions. The University Center for International Studies (UCIS) offers survey courses on the Soviet Union, Eastern Europe, modern Middle East, Africa, China, Japan, and Latin America. These are interdisciplinary and team taught and provide an introduction to the areas' culture, politics, economics, and geography. UCIS oversees undergraduate add-on certificate programs in global or area studies, administered by the director of the UCIS and by the individual area program directors in East Asian, Latin-American, Middle Eastern, and Slavic and East European studies. The Mershon Center presents courses in national security policies, among other international topics.

The university participates in such study-abroad activities as the summer program at Oxford University, and the programs in Mexico and Quebec under the auspices of the Committee on Institutional Cooperation. The Slavic Department, in cooperation with Purdue University, operates a Russian language program at the Pushkin Institute in Moscow. These are open to qualified students on a national basis. Study-tour programs from all parts of the university are organized on an ad hoc basis each year. These are generated by individual professors. The Center for Slavic and East European Studies, federally funded since 1965, also has an annual allocation of language and area fellowships. The East Asian and Middle Eastern programs are also recipients of graduate fellowships.

Ohio State has individualized instruction in foreign languages (IIFL) programs in Arabic, French, German, Latin, Russian, and Spanish. This is the largest program of its kind in the United States.

HOW ORGANIZED. The most important components of IIFL are contained in the acronym TAMBSPI (teacher-assisted, mastery-based, self-paced instruction). Though students work with specially prepared instructional materials, a teacher is available in a learning center to answer questions, organize informal conversation groups, etc. Students earn one credit at a time and proceed to the next unit after passing a unit test at 80 percent or better.

In language courses where both classroom and TAMBSPI programs are offered, approximately 25 percent of the enrollment is in TAMBSPI. For French or Spanish, offered at virtually every hour each quarter, the proportion is about 20 percent; but for Arabic, which starts a regular class only once a year, the figure is 71 percent.

The development of materials for the six languages was made possible by a major grant from the National Endowment for the Humanities, with the costs shared by the university. Now the program is permanent and funded entirely by the university. For a language like Arabic it is less expensive than regular classroom instruction. Students may transfer from the classroom section into TAMBSPI at any time and receive credit for classroom work already done. In many cases TAMBSPI may be the last stop before the student drops the language, but it is one way of saving those who normally would be lost to the program. TAMBSPI meets the needs of students who have scheduling problems, who learn languages at a pace faster or slower than that of the classroom, or who simply enjoy working on their own.

EDUCATIONAL IMPACT. NEH funds partially defrayed the costs of developing the first three courses in five languages and the first two in German. The success of these programs induced the College of Humanities to invest in the development of additional materials for one French and one Arabic (enough to meet the language requirement) and three additional courses in Russian. There are plans for more courses in German and Spanish and for new programs in Persian, Turkish, Polish, Serbo-Croatian, Chinese, and Japanese.

RESOURCE PERSON. Leon I. Twarog, Center for Slavic and East European Studies, 344 Dulles Hall, The Ohio State University, Columbus, OH 43210. Phone: (614) 422-8770/6733.

OHIO UNIVERSITY, Athens, OH

The university was established in 1804 as the first higher education institution in the Northwest Territory. Enrollment on the main Athens campus is approximately 14,000, while the 4 regional campuses and academic centers in southern Ohio enroll an additional 5,500. Full-time faculty number over 800. Bachelor's degrees are offered in over 150 areas, master's in 46, and doctorates in 16. The university is accredited by the North Central Association of Colleges and Secondary Schools and by the recognized professional accrediting associations identified with its major academic divisions. While a majority live in Ohio, students come from every state and from 75 other countries. This diversity adds a special dimension to the largely residential, small-town nature of the main campus.

INTERNATIONAL ASPECTS OF THE CURRICULUM. The commitment to international education at Ohio University is strong and growing, as evidenced in the size of the international student community (about 10 percent of the total student body); in exchange agreements with universities in Asia, Africa, and the Middle East; and, most recently, in the adoption of a general education requirement for all students that includes a Third World cultures dimension. A focal point for much of this activity is the Center for International Studies, established in 1969 to coordinate many of the university's international activities. The center is directed by the assistant provost for international studies, who is a member of the Dean's Council and who reports directly to the provost (chief academic officer). The center includes area studies programs in Africa, Latin America, and Southeast Asia. It offers baccalaureate and master's degrees as well as an undergraduate certificate in area studies. There are 24 students enrolled in the bachelor's program and 125 in the master's program.

Faculty and courses associated with the center are located in the traditional departments and schools. The center offers a few broad multidisciplinary courses (e.g., Modern Africa, Survey of Latin America) and also provides language instruction in Hausa, Arabic, Swahili, Indonesian, and, in cooperation with the Department of Modern Languages, Chinese.

General study abroad information is provided by the center, both on programs operated by Ohio University (largely through the Department of Modern Languages) and on those of other universities and organizations.

HOW ORGANIZED. There are four major undergraduate curricular dimensions to the work of the Center for International Studies. First is the major in international studies, which requires (in addition to general education and arts and science requirements) 52 quarter hours of work, including 16 in international relations or cross-cultural studies and 36 focusing on a single world region. Second, entering freshmen must take credits chosen from four or five general areas, one of which is Third World Cultures; a number of courses have been approved by the General Education Council to fulfill this requirement. Third, language instruction is offered in modern as well as less commonly taught languages and has been integrated with area studies. Fourth, many courses in the international and foreign studies areas are offered by several departments; a number of these contribute to the area studies programs. These programs are evaluated every five years by the University Curriculum Council.

EDUCATIONAL IMPACT. International education is an integral part of Ohio University, as evidenced by the many cooperative agreements with institutions abroad involving, among others at Ohio, the colleges of education, business administration, arts and sciences, engineering and technology, and fine arts. The Third World component of the general education requirement, various study-abroad programs, a large and active international student population, and a number of special events (such as the annual World Communication Conference and the Athens International Film Festival) indicate Ohio University's commitment to international education. The Center for International Studies is one part of this total involvement.

RESOURCE PERSON. Edward Baum, Assistant Provost and Director, Center for International Affairs, Ohio University, Athens, OH 45701. Phone: (614) 594-6039.

PACIFIC LUTHERAN UNIVERSITY, Tacoma, WA

Pacific Lutheran University (PLU) was founded in 1890 as an academy for the children of Scandinavian and German pioneers associated with the Lutheran Church in the Pacific Northwest. The school became a four-year liberal arts college in 1941 and a university in 1960. It enrolls 3,168 undergraduates and 308 master's-level graduate students in education, humanities, social sciences, business administration, music, and public administration. It has 204 full-time and 65 part-time faculty, of whom 60 percent have doctorates. The university's annual budget is $20.3 million, and it has an endowment equivalent to $5.6 million. Half of all PLU freshmen graduate.

INTERNATIONAL ASPECTS OF THE CURRICULUM. PLU has developed a comprehensive international education program to expand students' understanding of the global condition. This program entails three interrelated aspects. First are intensive multidisciplinary major-minor programs in global and international area studies. The most recent is the Foreign Area Studies Program (FASP), a comprehensive, integrated major-minor that combines global issues with area studies and includes language and study abroad. It begins with a required introductory Global Perspectives course, followed by course clusters on areas (Asia, Third World, Europe, and Scandinavia) and on issues (development and modernization; global resources and international trade; revolution, war, and peace; and cultures and traditions), drawing on courses from 12 departments or schools (anthropology, business administration, economics, education, history, modern and classical languages, philosophy, political science, psychology, sociology, religion, and the Integrated Studies Program). Students must focus on one area and one issues course cluster. The program culminates in an integrative seminar/project abroad. Two thematic minors within FASP are international trade for business majors and international affairs for social science, humanities, and part-time students. A related major program is Scandinavian area studies, which includes Scandinavian languages and courses in eight departments. Altogether these major-minors enroll over 100.

Second is the extensive internationalization of the general curriculum. This has involved the inclusion in PLU's divisions of humanities, natural sciences, social sciences, and schools of business administration and education of over 60 new or revised courses reflecting international and intercultural concerns. Some 1,600 students enrolled this year, a 250 percent increase over last year. There has been steady growth since FASP initiated this effort in 1976.

Third are cocurricular programs that offer four categories of exchanges: Academic Programs Abroad, including a special London campus; Service Programs Abroad, projects of service in the Third World; Work-Study Abroad in Europe, with ten-week-long paid internships and jobs in the summer; and Study Tours during interim and summer terms. Additional activities include international studies symposia, lectures, and cultural and film festivals. Over 5,000 from the campus and the community have participated during the year.

HOW ORGANIZED. FASP and other international education programs are coordinated by the director of the Office of International Education (OIE), who devotes half time to this task. The director reports to the provost, who chairs the universitywide Advisory Council on International Programs; this is composed of administrators and academic heads, including the chair of the language department. The 1980-81 budget for international programs—including administrative, curricular, and cocurricular expenses, beyond regular departmental authorizations—is $111,400. Fully 53 percent of that budget now comes from internal sources, reflecting a goal set in 1976 to institutionalize the cost of international programs. This budgetary strength has been assisted by revenues from several outreach programs in international education for foreign students, for military at a nearby base, and for K-12 teachers. A most important structural element has been the diffusion of program courses and coordination throughout PLU's departments, divisions, and schools; courses have thus been internalized within departments and faculty and departmental support has been solidified. There are separate faculty coordinators and committees for FASP's area and issues course clusters, for the minors (the dean of the School of Business Administration coordinates FASP's international trade minor), and for the Scandinavian studies program. The director of OIE provides overall assistance, coordination, planning, and promotional support, as well as grants for programs and faculty. Formal evaluation and institutional research is coordinated by PLU's Center for Human Organization in Changing Environments.

EDUCATIONAL IMPACT. The international education programs, in adding global issues to the general undergraduate curriculum, have had an impact on attitudes and values at PLU. Students have developed a more mature and diverse perspective while acquiring multidisciplinary skills that help them comprehend and analyze complex global issues. Institutionally, the integrative, multidisciplinary curriculum has pulled together compartmentalized faculty and generated programs that form a coherent, cross-fertilizing structure. Special results have been the beginning internationalization of business offerings, the development of preservice and inservice global studies courses within the School of Education, and increasing interest in the study of languages. Outreach has always been a feature of PLU's program; the university helped form the Pacific Northwest International/Intercultural Education Consortium, made up of 31 two- and four-year public and private institutions in Alaska, British Columbia, Washington, and Oregon. This arrangement includes cross-registration and articulation agreements with some of the consortium members. A recent large grant to support Citizen Education for Cultural Understanding has allowed PLU to help train some 234 consortium faculty at 13 institutions in global studies. This effort complements PLU's inservice training courses for K-12 teachers and BA and MA programs at the nearby military base.

RESOURCE PERSON. Mordechai Rozanski, Director, Office of International Education, Pacific Lutheran University, Tacoma, WA 98447. Phone: (206) 383-7628.

POMONA COLLEGE, Claremont, CA

The founding member of the Claremont Colleges, Pomona is an independent four-year coeducational liberal arts and preprofessional institution begun in 1887. Of 1,300 students 90 percent live on campus and 6 percent are international students; with a staff of 130 the student-faculty ratio is 11 to 1. There are 29 concentrations in the humanities, natural sciences, and social sciences. Pomona's 1980-81 freshman class has median SAT scores of 600 verbal and 630 math. Tuition is $5,470; room and board is $2,320. In 1979-80 over $3 million in financial aid was given to 46 percent of students. Recent annual educational and general expenditures were over $15.5 million on total assets over $129.3 million. Of the 1980 graduating class 38 percent are enrolled in graduate and professional schools.

INTERNATIONAL ASPECTS OF THE CURRICULUM. Pomona's programs in international relations, modern languages, and education abroad all utilize the *Oldenborg Center for Modern Languages and International Relations*, which combines learning and social environments in a modern residence hall. Built for this purpose in 1966, the center houses 140 students from all 4 classes (one eighth of Pomona's resident students). It sponsors a variety of international, intercultural, and language activities involving a large portion of the college community.

The international relations major (supervised and taught by an interdisciplinary faculty committee) combines languages, study abroad, economics, politics, history, anthropology, area studies, and an interdisciplinary approach to social sciences. The number of majors has increased to about 100, or 8 percent of the student body. Many more students in other majors (such as economics and government) focus on international concerns.

Claremont students may study more than a dozen languages. In Pomona's Department of Modern Languages and Literatures most courses are taught in the target language. Students may major in one language; in Asian, Latin-American, or Russian studies; in linguistics; in foreign languages; or in foreign literatures (the latter two require at least two languages). About 50 students are majoring in these subjects.

Approximately one third of Pomona's students participate in the Education Abroad Program in more than 20 countries. Students from all majors select from among the Pomona programs in Oxford, Paris, Madrid, Geneva, and Jerusalem. Others choose field tutorials led by Pomona professors, independent study, or other affiliated programs. Emphasis is on teaching by natives of the host country, supervised field work, and involvement in the host culture. Students generally pay the same amount as they would on campus and receive their normal financial aid. Overseas transportation is provided. The college meets all costs of the Education Abroad Program, including overseas salaries and administration, from tuition and other revenues.

HOW ORGANIZED. The Oldenborg Center is supervised by the director (a full-time administrator with faculty rank who reports to the vice president for academic affairs), an assistant director, and five native language residents who live in the dormitories with the students (90 percent American). There are many activities for the five language sections (French, Spanish, German, Russian, and Mandarin Chinese), such as films, plays, lectures, ethnic meals, and weekly study breaks. Original taped language programs may be monitored in each student's room. About 200 Claremont students and faculty at all levels of fluency meet on weekdays to practice two dozen languages informally. Students may register for cumulative academic credit (one half course per year) on a pass/no credit basis for attendance at center language activities and intermediate and advanced conversation classes held twice a week by the language residents. To encourage wider participation many events are held in English, especially the International Relations Colloquium, a speakers' program.

Although the building was donated, annual operating costs are met out of the college budget. In addition to paying salaries (the five language residents each receive $5,000 plus room and board), the college allots funds for films, speakers, faculty meals, supplies, and equipment.

EDUCATIONAL IMPACT. Furthering international awareness has long been a goal of Pomona College. Its emphasis on international education began in the twenties, when Charles Edmunds came from a Chinese university to assume the presidency. His successors (E. Wilson Lyon, 1941-69, and David Alexander), both Rhodes scholars, continued to encourage international programs. Alexander has been named American secretary of the Rhodes Scholarship Trust.

The international education programs are designed to involve every student and faculty member. Many nonmajors participate. Results of the tradition of encouraging an international outlook are impressive: At least 75 percent of each graduating class is involved in international studies. More than a third of the 1980 class took more foreign language study than the required three semesters. A third of the graduates took two or more languages; 7 percent took three or more.

RESOURCE PERSON. Cecilia C. Baumann, Director, Oldenborg Center, Pomona College, Claremont, CA 91711. Phone: (714) 621-8018.

RAMAPO COLLEGE OF NEW JERSEY, Mahwah, NJ

Ramapo College is a four-year liberal arts institution located in northern New Jersey. It opened in September 1971 as part of the state's overall plan to augment and improve its higher educational program. The college received full accreditation from the Middle States Association in 1975. It has 4,500 undergraduates and 160 full-time and 50 part-time faculty, with 85 percent holding doctoral or equivalent degrees. There are six interdisciplinary schools (American and international studies, administration and business, contemporary arts, environmental studies, social science and human services, and theoretical and applied sciences), two divisions (physical education and learning skills), and evening and Saturday extension programs. The college's annual budget is approximately $10 million.

INTERNATIONAL ASPECTS OF THE CURRICULUM. International education was designated one of the college's primary missions in the New Jersey 1980 Statewide Plan for Higher Education. Ramapo instituted a new interdisciplinary major in the School of American and International Studies. AIS students can major in political science (domestic, comparative, international), history (American, European), literature (American, world), or interdisciplinary American studies, with options for an international relations concentration. In September 1981 all incoming AIS students will be required to take a revised 16-credit core package providing both domestic and comparative education. They will then choose between the traditional disciplines and the new AIS major in one of its three tracts: international studies, American studies, and the business co-major. International studies carries requirements in languages, comparative/international politics, history, economics, and literature. In the business co-major there are similar requirements, along with electives specifically designed for those students.

Other activities complement Ramapo's basic international curriculum. For several years the college has utilized American University Field Staff personnel, who cover a wide range of topics particularly relevant to AIS. In 1980 Ramapo joined the College Consortium for International Studies (CCIS) and is already sponsoring study-abroad semesters in Ireland, as well as utilizing programs in other countries sponsored by other member schools. Additionally, mini-study-abroad courses during intersession periods are offered on credit and noncredit bases. Finally, the college accommodates about 70 foreign students each year from several countries, including France, Nigeria, China, and Japan. In response to growing demand for language training, Ramapo is upgrading the curriculum and introducing total immersion programs in French and Spanish in summer 1981.

HOW ORGANIZED. The supervision of Ramapo's international curriculum rests mainly with the director of the School of American and International Studies, the assistant director, and the unit curriculum committee. An AIS faculty member with release time coordinates participation with CCIS and, together with a unit screening committee, administers study-abroad programs. The college's director of interdisciplinary studies in the Office of Academic Affairs oversees the American University Field Staff program on an all-college basis, with an annual budget of $35,000.

EDUCATIONAL IMPACT. Ramapo's initiatives in international education correspond to growing national and state interest in this area and have received considerable faculty and student support. Comments on the new American and international studies interdisciplinary major routinely emphasize its comprehensive integration and clearer structure. AIS and the School of Business find great promise in the business co-major, in providing Ramapo undergraduates with unique education combinations in business, languages, politics, economics, history, and cultures. Students from all schools of the college are applying for study-abroad programs at a growing rate.

RESOURCE PERSON.   Andrea J. Simon, School of American and International Studies, Ramapo College of New Jersey, Mahwah, NJ 07430. Phone: (201) 825-2800, x554.

REED COLLEGE, Portland, OR

Reed was founded in 1911 as an independent, nonsectarian, coeducational liberal arts college. It has about 1,200 students, 110 faculty, and 125 staff. Students come from all parts of the country and from abroad. The college stresses a demanding science curriculum and a central concentration on interdisciplinary humanities courses. Most teaching is conducted in conferences of 15 to 25 students. Reed offers a BA in 21 departmental majors, 13 interdisciplinary majors (including international studies), and such special interdisciplinary programs as the faculty approves for individual students. An MA in liberal studies is also offered. About 45 percent of Reed graduates continue in graduate and other professional schools.

INTERNATIONAL ASPECTS OF THE CURRICULUM. The *international studies* (IS) interdisciplinary major was established for students interested in international affairs. The faculty directing the major form the International Studies Committee and represent the departments of history, political science, economics, and anthropology. Student programs are constructed from an approved list of courses in those departments (plus sociology), in consultation with IS Committee faculty advisors. Thus no separate budget has been necessary for the staffing or curriculum of the major. Reflecting college offerings and faculty interests, student programs tend to concentrate in studies of international relations and of economic and social development of new nations. The committee usually numbers about five; there are ten to twelve juniors and seniors in the major.

International studies majors must meet requirements beyond those of the college for the BA: two year-long sequences (usually an introductory course plus an upper-division course) chosen from anthropology, humanities, sociology, economics, political science, and history; six semester courses from the approved IS list, with no more than three in any one discipline; a Junior Qualifying Examination at the end of the junior year—usually a short essay, bibliography, and oral examination on the student's proposed senior thesis topic, or related subject; a senior thesis—a comprehensive research study between 50 and 150 pages (on a topic of the student's choice, approved by his advisor), defended at the end of the senior year in an oral examination; and a language requirement, which can be met in a variety of ways (course study, standard national examination, special examination by the IS Committee).

The intent is to give each student a grounding in appropriate disciplines before proceeding to an integrated and focused upper-division program. Most IS students take three rather than two introductory sequences, and more than the required number of additional courses.

HOW ORGANIZED. To be admitted to the IS major, students (usually in the sophomore year) petition the IS Committee, noting the problem or issues on which they intend to focus and explaining why a normal departmental major would not meet their goals. They outline their courses of study (including proposed courses) for the junior and senior years.

The six semesters of core courses are drawn from appropriate offerings from approved departments. Each year the faculty committee reviews the list to provide the broadest possible coverage of offerings relevant to international studies. Each student's program is intended to have a coherent focus while pursuing the goal of enhanced global understanding through interdisciplinary means. The senior thesis is closely monitored by the committee and the thesis advisor. Some students take one or two semesters of study abroad under various arrangements, and this work is integrated into their IS programs.

EDUCATIONAL IMPACT. The international studies major is an accepted and permanent part of the Reed curriculum. Its impact is out of proportion to the small number of majors—partly because the program, requiring high intellectual independence and interdisciplinary skill, attracts very able and motivated students. Reed is strongly interdisciplinary and interdepartmental in any case, due to such factors as the humanities program and the divisional organization of the college (e.g., history and social sciences, mathematics and natural sciences, language and literature). The IS program adds to this interdepartmental orientation; all IS faculty are members of the History and Social Science Division, although as the IS Committee they function separately. Reed students generally are interested in international affairs and IS students and faculty express this in various extracurricular ways. The IS faculty are also most active in bringing their expertise to the community (educational TV, forums, lectures, etc.).

RESOURCE PERSON. Chairman, International Studies Committee (through spring 1981, David Groff), Reed College, Portland, OR 97202. Phone: (503) 771-1112.

ROCKLAND COMMUNITY COLLEGE, Suffern, NY

Rockland (RCC) is an affiliated unit under the State University of New York and is sponsored by the legislature of Rockland County. Its degree programs are registered by the New York department of education, approved by the State University, and accredited by the Middle States Association of Colleges and Secondary Schools. The college awards the associate in arts and the associate in applied science and offers postsecondary programs combining general and technical education, including special courses and extension work. Operating costs are shared by New York state, Rockland County, and tuition. There are about 6,000 full-time students, 150 regular faculty, and part-time faculty from many professional fields. Rockland has a main campus and several community-based learning centers. Because of affiliations with many businesses, agencies, and organizations, and extensive international programs, there is a wide range of settings and instructional modes.

INTERNATIONAL ASPECTS OF THE CURRICULUM. Over the last decade RCC has developed a Global Agenda for Community Colleges in order to assess each aspect of institutional life for its international dimensions. This includes curricular and extracurricular aspects, the community service program, students, faculty, study/work/service abroad, and links with colleges and universities overseas. Three units help make the Global Agenda: the Rockland Centre for International Studies, International College, and the Center for International Students.

Since 1969 the Rockland Centre for International Studies has offered study/work/service programs around the world. Much of this is done in conjunction with the College Consortium for International Studies, which Rockland helped found. Programs include structured service-learning and independent study featuring the learning contract method, as well as many courses at overseas colleges and universities.

International College (IC) was created in 1976 to bring together curricular programs with international dimensions. It uses two-year curricula in religious, ethnic, and area studies that allow students to organize programs around these focuses in arts and sciences. Christian, Judaic and Israeli studies, and Irish studies have been established, and Italian studies and international business have been developed. IC houses foreign language and literature programs and is developing a small-class approach for less commonly taught languages, where conventional instruction proves inefficient. IC also works with the Office of Cultural Affairs to create public programs with international dimensions; with the Division of Community Service hold public policy forums on global issues in conjunction with the U.S. State Department for Rockland County leaders and executives; and with the Global Concerns Committee, which offers opportunities to explore international/intercultural issues.

The Center for International Students provides traditional services for 200 international students and about 400 immigrants or others weak in English so that they may fully benefit from their Rockland experience. It also coordinates the international clubs (African, Haitian, Israeli, etc.), providing social and educational activities which permit RCC international students to be teaching resources.

HOW ORGANIZED. The Centre for International Studies is headed by the director of international education, who also is liaison for the College Consortium for International Studies. RCC's program in Israel is the best developed of the overseas programs, with over 200 going to Israel each semester to some 38 colleges, universities, and informal settings. Rockland serves as the consortium agent for this program. The director works closely with RCC academic departments to discover interests and needs that can be met by strengthening programs or by creating new ones. The director administers all aspects of the study/work/service abroad programs.

International College's two-year associate in arts program allows students to meet general education requirements and electives while focusing on international/intercultural concerns. Its core includes an interdisciplinary English and social science year studying the concept of culture through literature integrated with anthropological and sociological themes, and language studies related to the student's area of special interest. In addition to typical language offerings, IC has a self-study language center which provide readings, tapes, native-speaking tutors, and access to some 30 languages. In the first year the student concentrates on a special interest—ethnic/cultural heritage, religion, world region, global problem, language, or international service preparation. Ideally the first semester is on campus, the second moves the student into community experiences, and the last two are abroad. IC has been moving strongly toward service learning, whereby students in local communities or abroad integrate community-based service into their studies.

EDUCATIONAL IMPACT. Rockland's Global Agenda enjoys support from the county legislature, from RCC's board of trustees, and almost universally from the college. Faculty have become so involved in study-abroad programs, in curriculum design at home, and in other international activities that more want to become involved than can easily be accommodated. External funding has been attracted and makes possible the widening of international dimensions throughout the curriculum. A U.S. Department of Education grant permits a larger group of faculty to develop international modules that can be infused into existing courses. This grant has also allowed the incorporation of work with a New York community college consortium and the creation of a national network of teachers exploring international curricula.

RESOURCE PERSON. Seymour Eskow, President, or Gerhard Hess, Director of International Education, Rockland Community College, 145 College Road, Suffern, NY 10901. Phone: (914) 356-4650.

ST. ANSELM'S COLLEGE, Manchester, NH

St. Anselm's is an accredited, coeducational, four-year liberal arts college founded in 1889 by the Order of St. Benedict. It enrolls 922 men and 691 women full time and 310 part-time students. It has 100 full-time and 45 part-time faculty. Undergraduate degrees offered: associate—police/law enforcement/corrections; bachelor's—biological sciences, business and management, education, languages, nursing, English, philosophy, theology, mathematics, physical sciences, psychology, social sciences (economics, history, geography, political science and government, sociology, urban studies). Humanities Program requirement. Almost 35 percent of 4-year program graduates enter graduate or professional studies. Special academic programs: use of native speakers in language programs, study abroad 3-2 liberal arts/career combination with Notre Dame in engineering, cross registration with New Hampshire College and University Council.

INTERNATIONAL ASPECTS OF THE CURRICULUM. In 1977 St. Anselm's College introduced a new core program, funded by the National Endowment for the Humanities—*Portraits of Human Greatness*. The program is a two-year lecture-seminar course required of all freshmen and sophomores. The program involves, in varying degrees, almost every discipline represented at St. Anselm's College and aims to significantly increase students' critical understanding of ideas and values—their own and those of other cultures, past and present. One aspect of this program is a focus on the study of languages, especially on use of the language, so that the student may study in depth at least one foreign culture. To ensure that students reach the necessary level of fluency for this program, St. Anselm's College utilizes a native speaker program. Every student enrolled in basic and intermediate language courses participates for one hour weekly in a small group (usually five students) led by a native speaker; the discussion is carried on entirely in the language being studied. This intensive approach to fluency, as well as the study of foreign cultures it makes possible, also prepares the student for a series of advanced electives in the general Humanities Program—the comparative culture courses (for example, one course compares Paris and New York in the 1920s and 1930s). The St. Anselm's approach to foreign language learning helps attract students to these courses. Since more than 500 students take part in the native speaker program, the St. Anselm's Humanities Program has a strong international orientation.

HOW ORGANIZED. In the native speaker groups, discussion materials include board games, magazine articles, art, music, and course work at the college. In advanced groups there is material from the student's major (groups are often organized according to field).

Because of the many sections required for the native speaker program, careful scheduling is vital, as is constant coordination of native speaker sessions with regular language courses. Native speakers need not treat precisely the same material as is covered by regular lecture sessions, but to avoid too wide a disparity, weekly staff meetings are essential. The language department schedules a weekly hour for evaluation and coordination of the two aspects of the program.

Although initially funded by the National Endowment for the Humanities, the native speaker program is now financed entirely by the college; its success and positive impact on the liberal arts program at St. Anselm's ensure a permanent place in the curriculum.

EDUCATIONAL IMPACT. The native speaker program has been widely praised by faculty and is seen as making a significant contribution to the students' liberal education, helping them to acquire a more objective, critical view of their own culture. The development of the native speaker program as a part of the broader Humanities Program has also helped integrate language faculty with other liberal arts faculty, and has thus created opportunities for interdisciplinary cooperation both within and outside the Humanities Program. Students have also been enthusiastic; despite the rigor of the native speaker program, a poll indicated that 86 percent of students preferred the approach to more traditional language study methods. This spirit is reflected in test scores; on language achievement tests St. Anselm's students now score significantly higher than they did before the program began.

RESOURCE PERSON. John D'Espinosa, Chairman, Modern Languages Department, St. Anselm's College, Manchester, NH 03102. Phone: (603) 669-1030, x311.

ST. EDWARD'S UNIVERSITY, Austin, TX

St. Edward's is a Catholic, independent, coeducational university. The curriculum emphasizes critical reasoning, communication skills, and values clarification. The BA, BS, and bachelor of business administration are awarded. Undergraduate classes are offered in day and evening. The master of business administration and MA in human services are offered through evening classes. The New College provides a program for those who are 25 or older that leads to the bachelor of liberal studies. More than 2,200 students from 44 states and 32 other countries attend St. Edward's.

INTERNATIONAL ASPECTS OF THE CURRICULUM. The *Global Studies Program* enables the university to reflect world realities in the classroom—to produce graduates who understand that African, Asian, and Latin-American nations no longer tolerate ethnocentric and paternalistic relations with industrial countries. The objective is to help students grasp the nature of global interdependence and develop sensitivity to Third World peoples and cultures.

The program is designed to complement traditional majors and career education. Its curriculum involves a core of 18 credits including anthropology, two Third World studies seminars, and the histories of Asia, Africa, and Latin America. Global Studies is not a major, but leads to certification.

A significant part of the program is an internship in a Third World location. This follows academic preparation and is a closely supervised learning experience related to the student's major. Each internship is structured to meet the needs of the student and of the host. Ideally this semester-long phase occurs during the spring term of the junior year or the fall term of the senior year.

HOW ORGANIZED. The program is administered by one faculty member, in conjunction with regular teaching responsibilities, who works with an interdisciplinary faculty committee that oversees its curriculum. As Global Studies is a permanent part of the university, it has no special budget. The faculty coordinator is generally located in the Department of Behavioral and Social Sciences.

Most Global Studies students intern in Latin America; the program is being expanded to Africa and Asia. The student is placed in a situation paralleling career goals. For example, a prelaw student worked with several attorneys in Bogotá, Colombia, being tutored in the country's judicial system. Visits to courts, penal institutions, and inland villages, as well as a supervised academic segment, helped the intern grasp Colombia's problems in particular and Third World problems in general.

Students must be proficient in the appropriate language in order to go abroad. Deficient students attend one of the language facilities in Cuernavaca, Mexico, before taking Latin-American internships. As the program expands in Africa and Asia, similar intensive language learning arrangements will be established. Students absorb the cost of their internships, including travel and subsistence. They usually live with a family for about $7 per day. Generally the cost of the Latin-American semester has not exceeded that of being on campus in Austin; in many cases it has been less expensive.

EDUCATIONAL IMPACT. Returning interns have significant effect on campus academic life. The program, along with the presence at St. Edward's of international students, has engendered a new awareness in all faculty and students. A curriculum mix requiring an intercultural understanding of developing countries and of interdependence, as well as competence in the appropriate language, is believed to educate citizens who comprehend world complexities. Since Global Studies is a concentration taken in conjunction with a traditional major, a greater number of students is reached.

RESOURCE PERSON. Don E. Post, Director, Global Studies, St. Edward's University, 3001 South Congress Avenue, Austin, TX 78704. Phone: (512) 444-2621.

ST. OLAF COLLEGE, Northfield, MN

St. Olaf College, founded in 1874 by Norwegian-Lutheran pastors, farmers, and businessmen, is affiliated with the American Lutheran Church. It was one of the first colleges in the nation to adopt the 4-1-4 calendar. The St. Olaf Paracollege, within the general college, provides an optional study opportunity based on the British tutorial system. St. Olaf has 3,000 resident students and a full-time faculty of 200. The college draws students from most states, although the majority are from the Midwest. Majors are available in more than 50 areas.

INTERNATIONAL ASPECTS OF THE CURRICULUM. St. Olaf offers about 25 semester- or year-abroad programs and a dozen interim-term-abroad courses, all directly sponsored by the college. An additional eight consortium programs for overseas study are available to St. Olaf students. Included in the study-abroad opportunities are five language programs (Chinese, French, German, Spanish, and Norwegian), six semester- or year-abroad programs in England, and a number of individual study-service programs in developing countries. There are three supervised five-month programs abroad (semester and interim), each enrolling twenty to thirty per year; these programs are Far East (one month in Taiwan and four in Thailand), Middle East (four months in Israel and one in Turkey, Greece, and Rome), and global (see below). For each of these latter programs, a St. Olaf professor accompanies the students for the five-month period.

The Global Term Abroad takes students around the world, with visits to a number of countries in Europe, Africa, the Middle East, and Asia; the academic components are focused on four areas—Egypt, India, Taiwan, and Japan. The group spends a month in each country. The accompanying professor teaches one course in his or her discipline during the term abroad. The remaining four courses are taught with the assistance of coordinators in each of the four countries and in association with staff members of such institutions as American University in Cairo; the Ecumenical Christian Center, Bangalore, India; Soochow University in the National Palace Museum, Taipei, Taiwan; and Kyoto University in Japan.

The program course credits are in The Arts of China, Social Patterns and Development in India, Islamic-Egyptian History, and Religions of Japan. The 1980-81 St. Olaf-taught course is Comparative Economic Systems. The budget for the program covers all costs to the student other than incidental expenses; the 1980-81 global program charges were $2,610 beyond the comprehensive fee. The program is competitive and limited to 32 students.

HOW ORGANIZED. St. Olaf overseas programs are administered by the international studies office, staffed by a director and two and a half support staff. The director of international studies reports to the assistant dean of the college. The administrative expenses of the international studies office are supported by an international studies fee (currently $300 for a term abroad) assessed to each participating student. The remaining portion of the comprehensive fee is applied to the study-abroad program. If expenses exceed the comprehensive fee, the student pays the balance as a program fee. The college allows all financial aid to apply to off-campus programs.

All overseas study programs are approved by faculty vote. An international studies committee, composed of faculty, students, and administrators, is responsible for initial program review, program evaluation, and general policy development. Each program has a program advisor, appointed by the assistant dean, who is a faculty member in an appropriate discipline and is responsible for monitoring all academic components of the program. In addition, larger programs have a faculty advisory committee.

The college has given special attention to orientation of students prior to departure. Each spring there is a weekend retreat at a camp off campus, required for all students going abroad the next year. In addition, program advisors organize orientation sessions for their groups. As the majority of study-abroad programs are during the fall semester and interim term, a special "reentry day" is organized for returning students the day prior to the beginning of the next semester. There is a welcome back to campus, and special evaluation sessions are conducted with each returning group.

EDUCATIONAL IMPACT. International programs have had a significant impact on St. Olaf College and its students. Over half of St. Olaf graduates study overseas through the various opportunities. A large number of graduates have gone into international work, particularly in the mission field. Approximately 40 faculty have had at least one term-abroad experience because of involvement in an overseas study program. As evidence of the college's increased commitment to cross-cultural study, a cross-cultural international component was added to the curriculum two years ago. This requires all students to complete at least one course with an emphasis on Third World study.

RESOURCE PERSON. Lee M. Swan, Assistant Dean of the College, St. Olaf College, Northfield, MN 55057. Phone: (507) 663-3006.

THE SCHOOL FOR INTERNATIONAL TRAINING
Brattleboro, VT

The School for International Training (SIT), a specialized senior college and professional graduate school, is the accredited educational arm of The Experiment in International Living. Founded in 1967, it is located on a 200-acre semi-rural campus near Brattleboro, where some 225 students of its annual full-time equivalent enrollment of 700 are in residence at one time. The school evolved from The Experiment's extensive work with the Peace Corps. It has a full-time faculty of about 50. There are four master's programs, one junior-senior year bachelor's program, two transfer credit programs, and an intensive program in English as a second language for foreign students. Programs are alternative and experience based, with students moving through the curriculum in program groups, working with staff and other students on designing projects and solving problems. The Experiment's language teaching capability includes over 50 tongues; since 1964 Experiment linguists have developed texts to teach over a dozen exotic languages. Emphasis on work experience (either teaching assignments or internships) reflects SIT's commitment to experiential education.

INTERNATIONAL ASPECTS OF THE CURRICULUM. The curriculum, coupled with work experience overseas, is designed to expose students to careers in intercultural settings and to stimulate an understanding of complex international issues, a command of other languages, the capacity to live and work in other cultures, and an awareness of interdependence among nations and peoples.

The *World Issues Program* is a self-contained, multidisciplinary, junior and senior year program for students who want to make an international internship the focal point of their undergraduate studies.

World Issues organized its curriculum and the internship abroad around the following transnational fields of study: environmental quality, community and social development, economic development, intercultural communication, and peace studies. About 30 World Issues students in each entering class work to develop the skills and understanding necessary for professional involvement in these fields through direct participation in them.

To a degree not often found in undergraduate activity, this program integrates rigorous, disciplined, liberal arts study with work experience. The program enables students to achieve their goals through intensive orientation to living and working abroad, combining academic and practical experience, professional work during the overseas interval, intensive exploration of world problems, and cross-cultural and language studies. An important dimension of World Issues is concentration on students' personal and emotional growth. The intensive small-group nature of the program demands that students develop the inner resources necessary for interpersonal relations and for constructive work with groups. This challenge continues to influence students during the off-campus interval, when they face similar situations within established organizations in other cultures.

HOW ORGANIZED. A director supervises the World Issues Program. There is a faculty of five full-time teachers, who draw on resources from elsewhere in the school and from outside. The program is budgeted separately and is one of a half dozen semi-autonomous programs that make up SIT. The curriculum is divided into an initial on-campus period of 23 weeks, an internship abroad of 30 or more weeks, and an on-campus interval of final review and analysis of about 13 weeks.

The initial on-campus period includes courses in the five transnational fields indicated, plus professional skills development (resumes, job interviews, career decisions, organizational skills), intensive language study, and internship preparation (analytical skills, project proposals and evaluation). Regular, frequent meetings with advisors result in the drafting of an individual internship curriculum called a Learning Contract which, after review by the entire faculty, serves as a guide for the student's off-campus work and learning.

In the internship period students work as beginning (or, occasionally, middle-level) professionals with such organizations as Save the Children, Indonesia; United Nations *Development Forum*, Switzerland; National Park Service of Costa Rica; Ministry of Agriculture, Egypt; Island Resources Foundations, Virgin Islands; Amnesty International, Austria and the U.S.; Peace Corps Language Development, Botswana; Women's International Information Communication Service, Italy; American Friends Service Committee, Puerto Rico; and Ministry of Health, Planning Division, Monrovia, Liberia.

In the final on-campus period students concentrate on analysis of the internship experience and develop further understanding of the theoretical bases of their fields. Discussion with faculty of specific opportunities for advanced study or employment also constitute an important element of this concluding phase of the undergraduate program.

EDUCATIONAL IMPACT. As the undergraduate version of several similarly designed degree programs at SIT, the World Issues Program represents a way of learning that most students find intellectually invigorating and many find difficult, but that no student finds lacking in integrity or potential for growth. Because of the nature of The Experiment and SIT, the international dimension constitutes the curriculum. The impact on undergraduates is reflected even before graduation in such extracurricular activities as participation in student foreign affairs conferences and Model UNs around the United States. SIT also conducts the College Semester Abroad program for sophomores, juniors, and seniors from other U.S. colleges and universities; several hundred participate around the world in these 15-week programs and are thus exposed to SIT's approach to international education.

RESOURCE PERSON. Shaun Bennett, Director, World Issues Program, School for International Training, Kipling Road, Brattleboro, VT 05301. Phone: (802) 257-7751.

SPELMAN COLLEGE, Atlanta, GA

Spelman was founded in 1881 to improve educational opportunities for black women in the South. The basic educational work of the early years was vocational and remedial; the first college degree was conferred in 1901, and in 1924 Spelman became a full liberal arts college. With Morehouse College and Atlanta University, Spelman formed the Atlanta University Center Corporation in 1929; three other neighboring institutions (Clark College, Morris Brown College, and the Interdenominational Theological Center) joined later. Students may cross register and several programs are shared among institutions. Spelman has 1,250 students (800 of whom reside on campus), 90 full-time faculty, and an endowment of almost $20 million.

INTERNATIONAL ASPECTS OF THE CURRICULUM. Spelman conducts three interrelated international programs: an international and intercultural element of the core curriculum; a minor in transcultural studies; and a lecture and visitors program on world issues and cultures for the Spelman community. Faculty from all sections of the college have participated in these international programs.

The fundamental international part of the core curriculum is the mandatory two-semester course, *World Civilizations*. It is designed to demonstrate the rise and influence of Europe but also to introduce students to the contributions of Asian and African cultures. The cross-cultural sharing that has gone on for centuries is given great emphasis. Students must also take four semesters of language. Spanish and French are offered at Spelman; Chinese, German, Russian, and Swahili may be taken at other institutions within the Atlanta University Center. At the sophomore level of the core, students may take various departmental courses that deepen the intercultural approach of World Civilizations. In addition to African art and European drama, courses in the history and appreciation of music, principles of economics, anthropology, and many others have large non-American and non-European components and build on the work accomplished in World Civilizations.

The *transcultural studies* minor program consists of 18 to 21 credits of designated courses beyond the World Civilization and language requirements and must be taken in at least three departments outside the major. The capstone is a required six-credit seminar in transcultural studies taken at the junior or senior level and conducted by senior Spelman faculty with the cooperation of the Executive Council on Foreign Diplomats in America and the Fletcher School of International Law and Diplomacy of Tufts University.

At least four lectures per semester are given in the *Spelman International Forum*. Speakers have included top-level American diplomats such as Ambassador Donald McHenry, foreign writers and diplomats, and American scholars. These talks are integrated with core programs and transcultural studies.

Program courses are budgeted from college funds. The transcultural seminar is financed in its extracollegiate aspects by the Executive Council. The speakers series has been supported by Spelman, the Thurman Foundation, and the U.S. International Communications Agency.

HOW ORGANIZED. The World Civilizations course is in the history department and under the direction of the chairman. It is supervised by an interdepartmental committee which evaluates the syllabus and instruction. To achieve an interdisciplinary approach, faculty from departments other than history are used as lecturers and discussion group leaders. The college staffs the program only with permanent faculty highly ranked in yearly evaluations.

The minor and the International Forum are coordinated by the International Affairs Committee. Its chairman handles the details while the committee supervises the program, making broad policy decisions and evaluating its operation.

All programs are a permanent part of the curriculum. Even elements that use some outside funding can be modified if moneys are inadequate or agencies withdraw support.

EDUCATIONAL IMPACT.   Spelman's international programs have had a considerable effect on the college. Student awareness of foreign cultures and international issues has been enhanced. Attendance at extracurricular forums has steadily mounted since their inception. Faculty have become aware of the international dimensions of their studies. While social science faculty participated enthusiastically from the beginning, those in the natural sciences have not lagged. The interdisciplinary nature of World Civilizations and the minor have generated respect among faculty for other disciplines and a spirit of cooperation.

Cooperative programs with other institutions have enhanced the curriculum. Spelman faculty and students are encouraged to attend seminars and lectures sponsored by the Southern Center for International Studies. Students who want international careers may intern with the Atlanta Council for International Visitors; they have done research for the council, acted as interpreter-guides, made contacts for international visitors, and so on. The International Affairs Committee also encourages students to intern with such agencies as the U.S. State Department and with international sections of major corporations. Scholarships for overseas travel, one for a junior year abroad, and one following graduation are available. And Spelman cooperates with other Center institutions in fully funded programs of summer study in Haiti and the Dominican Republic.

RESOURCE PERSON.   Martin Yanuck, Box 21, Spelman College, Atlanta, GA 30314. Phone: (404) 681-4643, x212.

STANFORD UNIVERSITY, Stanford, CA

Founded in 1885, Stanford is one of the youngest major private universities in the world. Since it opened in 1896 it has grown to 1,205 full-time professors, almost 12,000 students (about 56 percent undergraduate and 44 percent graduate), a library of over 4.5 million volumes, an annual operating budget of $130 million, and an endowment of about $590 million. Since 1948 the university has been organized into seven schools: earth sciences, education, business, humanities and sciences, engineering, law, and medicine. In addition to students from every state (with about 40 percent of undergraduates from California), Stanford's enrollment includes about 1,700 foreign students from nearly 100 countries. They comprise less than 4 percent of undergraduates, about 25 percent of graduate students, and about 32 percent of postdoctoral scholars.

INTERNATIONAL ASPECTS OF THE CURRICULUM. *Stanford Overseas Studies*, established in 1958, is designed to give undergraduates, regardless of major, an extended and structured academic experience in a non-U.S. setting and culture. The program accommodates about 600 Stanford students each year in 12 locations for study periods ranging from 3 months to a year. Centers are in Vienna, Paris, Tours, Berlin, Haifa, Florence, Salamanca, and near London; in addition, Stanford students attend four interuniversity programs in Rome, Lima, São Paulo, and in several locations in Africa.

At some locations students enroll directly in a foreign university under the supervision of a Stanford faculty member; other programs provide a Stanford-designed curriculum, including intensive language instruction and courses on the country and culture in which the study center operates. Students in the foreign universities need at least two years of language training; for the other programs six months (two quarters) of training is required.

Students overseas pay the usual Stanford tuition and remain eligible for financial aid as regularly enrolled Stanford students making normal progress toward graduation. They come from all departments; over half the courses taught overseas provide credit toward departmental majors, and all courses provide credit toward graduation. Over one third of each graduating class has participated in the overseas studies program; in a recent survey 20 percent evaluated their experience as good and 68 percent as excellent.

The program's operating budget is about $2.5 million. The academic and administrative part is financed in the same way as in any departmental budget in the university.

The general curriculum centers overseas are staffed primarily by locally hired faculty under the supervision of a national and permanent resident director. A limited number of home campus faculty teach overseas each year for one or more quarters. Occasionally special academic programs focusing on a particular area of inquiry and using home campus faculty are offered to facilitate enrollment by students (especially those in scientific and technical fields) whose degree requirements might otherwise preclude study overseas.

HOW ORGANIZED. The curriculum overseas reflects the diversity of locations and wide range of student interests and levels of preparation. In the Stanford-designed curricula there is intensive daily language instruction and a choice of courses on literature, art, music, history, economics, politics, and other aspects of the local culture, as well as opportunities for directed reading and independent study. Academic field trips expand and elaborate on the courses. Students with sufficient language proficiency can audit some local university courses.

The programs that enroll students directly in foreign universities include on-site orientation programs of varying lengths and regular supervision by a member of the Stanford faculty in residence. Students are encouraged to take courses that complement their academic interests and goals, in order to acquire a different cultural perspective about a subject to which they have already been exposed.

Students from all programs are encouraged to build on their overseas experience on their return by consciously using their new perspectives in courses they select. Stanford is careful to offer opportunities overseas that can be supported academically by faculty depth and the curriculum on the home campus.

Ten staff members administer the program at Stanford and are advised by a student-faculty committee; the director reports to the provost of the university. Courses are evaluated by students (paralleling student course evaluation on campus), by the resident director, and by campus departments, which assess whether the course meets the requirements of a major. General program evaluation, through on-site visits and student and faculty debriefing, is ongoing.

EDUCATIONAL IMPACT. Stanford Overseas Studies is seen by students, faculty, and the university administration as one of Stanford's major strengths. The overseas courses expand the curriculum for all majors, particularly international relations, area studies, languages, and literature. Campus faculty pursue research and teaching interests outside the U.S., and occasional exchange of instructors strengthens basic language training.

Several language and cultural area student residences have been created in response to the interest of returned students, and they cooperate closely with Overseas Studies in providing orientation for students going overseas. In addition, they schedule films, lectures, and discussions about the cultural areas they represent. The many students with overseas experience provide audience and resources for these activities.

Several other Stanford-based programs provide overseas opportunities. Volunteers in Asia, a privately funded English-language teaching and appropriate-technology resource center, and the Interuniversity Language Programs in Tokyo and Taipei, provide Asian locations for language and area studies learning. The Bechtel International Center provides extensive information about study, work, and travel opportunities outside the U.S. as well as a varied program of activities for foreign students at Stanford.

RESOURCE PERSON. Mark Mancall, Director, Stanford Overseas Studies Program, PO Box L, Stanford, CA 94305. Phone: (415) 497-3555.

STATE UNIVERSITY OF NEW YORK AT ALBANY, Albany, NY

State University of New York at Albany is one of four university centers in the SUNY system. Founded in 1844, SUNYA enrolls 15,000 students in a wide variety of programs, including 45 leading to a bachelor's degree, 46 leading to a master's, and 22 leading to a doctorate. Albany encompasses nine degree-granting schools and colleges: humanities and fine arts, science and mathematics, social and behavioral sciences, business, criminal justice, education, library and information science, public affairs, and social welfare. The main (uptown) campus, on 500 acres at the western edge of Albany, features a 13-building "podium" with a common roof and connecting tunnels. The downtown campus includes residence, instruction, clinical, and research facilities and is served by free shuttle buses. More than three fourths of the 700-member faculty hold doctorates and many are international leaders in their fields.

INTERNATIONAL ASPECTS OF THE CURRICULUM. Because of its long tradition of strong language departments, Albany had emphasized through its *Office of International Programs* the development of study-abroad opportunities as an extension of on-campus courses, as well as student and faculty exchange programs. These remain the principal functions of the office. But since only a small percentage of students were being reached, an on-campus program in comparative cultures was created to provide global perspectives and an awareness of worldwide problems. The first step, in 1976, was a core course entitled *Cultural Diversity and Human Condition*.

Designed as an academic year course, it deals each semester with selected aspects of the cultures of three world areas, providing insight into the attitudes and behavior of six widely differing peoples. The cultural areas examined vary somewhat from year to year, depending on availability of faculty and the desire to introduce fresh material. Areas examined have included France, China, Iran, India, Mexico, Russia, Hausa or Ashanti regions (Nigeria), and Central America. The course is interdisciplinary and is team taught by faculty from the College of Humanities and Fine Arts and the College of Social and Behavioral Sciences. Departments represented are philosophy, French, Spanish, Chinese studies, Slavic studies, African and Afro-American studies, history, anthropology, and sociology. The course is offered without prerequisites and students may enroll in either semester independently. Although intended primarily for freshmen and sophomores, it also attracts upperclass students. It usually carries its maximum of 120 to 130 students, with the largest group from the business school.

During its first two years the course was partially supported by a grant from the U.S. Department of Education ($30,000 for 1976-77 and $28,000 for 1977-78). Since that time it has been entirely funded by the two participating colleges. Although initiated by the Office of International Programs, it is now officially listed as an interdisciplinary course with the designation Humanities 150a and b.

HOW ORGANIZED. Each semester begins with about a week of classes dealing with issues in intercultural interactions in the contemporary world, with some attempt at both exemplifying and modeling responsible styles of interaction at both personal and national levels. The course director coordinates the three segments, while each cultural area is the responsibility of a different faculty member. To provide continuity among the segments and to avoid superficiality, the same themes are examined for each cultural area—such as family relationships, educational objectives and practices, and the role of religion. Each segment is taught with the goal of promoting more responsible participation in international life, rather than merely providing information about other peoples. Each faculty member is responsible for student evaluation in his segment of the course.

The course teaches students to identify constituent features of the cultures studied and supports exploratory engagements (from a distance) with each. In addition to lectures, there is much student-faculty interaction, facilitated by microphones and electronic response systems at each student station. Frequent use is made of films, slides, and recordings. Students and faculty native to the area under consideration serve as resource people.

A student evaluation of the course is conducted at the end of each semester. The course is now established as a permanent part of the general curriculum.

EDUCATIONAL IMPACT. The varied efforts of the Office of International Programs, with activities in China, France, Germany, Israel, Japan, the Netherlands, Singapore, and the Soviet Union, along with plans for expanding the on-campus international components of the curriculum, have pointed to the need for a faculty advisory group. In fall 1979 an International Studies Council was appointed and charged with reviewing programs and advising on policy for the future development of international studies. The council is representative of the university.

The curriculum committee now has a new second field sequence (minor) in comparative cultures, with Humanities 150a or b as one of two requirements. A new interdisciplinary major in international studies has been designed as a pre-professional program for prospective graduate students in business or law. Students are strongly encouraged to earn a portion of the credits for both the second field and the major in study-abroad programs.

RESOURCE PERSON. Robert M. Garvin, Philosophy Department (Cultural Diversity and Human Condition) and Charles W. Colman, Director, Office of International Programs, State University of New York at Albany, 1400 Washington Avenue, Albany, NY 12222. Phone: (518) 457-8055 (Garvin)/457-8678 (Colman).

TARRANT COUNTY JUNIOR COLLEGE—NORTHEAST CAMPUS
Hurst, TX

The Tarrant County Junior College District was formed in 1965. The South Campus opened in 1967, the Northeast Campus in 1968, and the Northwest Campus in 1976. TCJC is an open-door comprehensive community college, providing a range of programs including developmental, general academic, technical-vocational, student development services, and community services. There are 20,798 students enrolled for credit courses in the TCJC District, a full-time equivalent (FTE) of 11,123, of whom 8,644 (FTE 4,504) are on the Northeast Campus. Faculty number 172 full time and 180 part time on this campus. About 8,000 students take noncredit courses on NE Campus yearly. The average student age is 28.

INTERNATIONAL ASPECTS OF THE CURRICULUM. The *Integrated Language Learning* program of the NE Campus Department of Foreign Languages emphasizes the development of language proficiency, with intensive language course work reinforced with courses in history, culture, and civilization to prepare students for basic language use, for comprehension of language as a component of culture, and for additional study at the university level. Three-year sequences are offered in French, German, and Spanish; one year of Russian is available. The credit curriculum in the three major languages includes 4 semesters (14 semester hours) of sequential basic language study, followed by 2 semesters (6 hours) of history, culture, and civilization. In addition, there are approximately 30 one-semester-hour courses in each language at 5 levels. Some reinforce various aspects of language learning, such as four levels of conversation, four levels of grammar review, two levels of listening comprehension, two levels of composition, multiple levels of reading, and linguistics. Others reinforce and supplement cultural instruction and add further international dimensions to the curriculum. Representative course titles are History of the Weimar Republic, Nazi Germany, Paris for Travelers, Mexico for Travelers, French Cooking, Barrio Spanish, Taboo French, Personal Correspondence, and Business Correspondence.

Extracurricular activities provide motivation for language learning and encourage identification with the international community. These include French wine- and cheese-tasting parties, foreign-language theatrical and musical performances, campus foreign film festivals, and annual travel with faculty to Mexico during spring vacation and to France in May.

The foreign languages credit program enrolls 850 students. Another 100 are in noncredit courses in conversational Spanish. In addition, 50 to 60 primary school children take the preparatory programs each semester in French and Spanish.

HOW ORGANIZED. The Department of Foreign Languages is one of five departments in the Humanities Division on Northeast Campus. Instruction is provided by four full-time and six to eight part-time faculty. All courses in the department are organized on a mastery model, with learning objectives and evaluation techniques specific for students. Tests are given on an individual, self-paced basis and are repeatable without penalty. Emphasis is on mastery of the objectives rather than on rigid time schedules. This has been in effect since 1970 and represents the instructional philosophy of the faculty.

Classes are taught primarily in the target language, with visual stimuli. Students practice independently in the language laboratory with cassette tapes, slide-tape presentations, filmstrips, videotapes, language master cards, sound-on-page documents, crossword puzzles, work sheets, and script manuals. Professional and peer tutors are available for one-to-one work. The lab is open 14 hours a day. It also functions as a testing center.

The instructional program is evaluated by enrollment trends, the percentage of completions, and grade distributions. Also, students regularly evaluate faculty performance. Since the initial outlay for laboratory and media equipment, the program functions on a budget of $1,200 to $1,800, plus $1,500 for replacement of media equipment and $2,000 to $3,000 for mediated instructional materials.

EDUCATIONAL IMPACT. The integrated language program has been well accepted, as evidenced by continued enrollment growth. On a campus with no language admission requirements and almost none for graduation, over 10 percent of students are enrolled in credit language courses. Also, many each semester enroll in the NE Campus language program while taking their other course work at a neighboring university. Some departments now list and recommend language electives for their majors, and a few, such as criminal justice, are beginning to require language study for graduation. Many faculty and counselors encourage students to take languages while at TCJC; some are taking courses themselves. Language is being accepted as a useful secondary skill for students desiring to add an international dimension to their life or career endeavors.

RESOURCE PERSON. Jane Harper, Chair, Department of Foreign Languages, NE Campus, Tarrant County Junior College, 828 Harwood Road, Hurst, TX 76053. Phone: (817) 281-7869, x400.

TEXAS SOUTHERN UNIVERSITY, Houston, TX

Texas Southern University was established by the Texas state legislature in 1947 as a senior-level institution offering bachelor's, master's, and doctoral degrees in nine schools. Degrees are conferred in the arts and sciences, teacher education, business, technology, public affairs, communications, pharmacy, and law. In 1973 the university was designated as a special-purpose institution for urban programming; many programs are designed to prepare students for service to the urban community. The library contains over 400,000 volumes, as well as the special Heartman Collection of books and periodicals by and about the Negro. The student body of 9,000 is multiethnic and multicultural. Most are from Texas; approximately 20 percent are international students from more than 50 countries. The multiethnic faculty numbers 420; 55 percent have doctorates. Most of the annual budget of about $20 million comes from state appropriations. A large majority of graduates pursue further studies.

INTERNATIONAL ASPECTS OF THE CURRICULUM. A strong commitment to international studies has been evident since the university was established. Courses in African, Latin-American, Asian, and European studies are offered in the College of Arts and Sciences, the School of Business, and the School of Public Affairs. In addition, majors are provided in French and Spanish and courses in German, Hausa, and Krio are offered.

An interdisciplinary concentration in international studies can be included in the degree program of any undergraduate. The concentration can be taken in African, Latin-American, Caribbean, or European studies; it consists of six semester hours of languages, twelve hours of international studies, and six hours of fine arts. The international courses are offered in several departments and are available to any student taking the international concentration curriculum. Students in the School of Business may include a concentration in international business, which consists of courses in international marketing, finance, economics, and appropriate technology for developing countries.

The university's general education curriculum in the humanities, social sciences, and natural sciences has been broadened by infusing international and intercultural studies into courses required of freshmen and sophomores. This has served to extend the student's basic knowledge of the world community.

International studies at Texas Southern University are enriched by summer study abroad for selected faculty and students. Through seminars, conferences, and workshops faculty development in international studies is enhanced and student knowledge of the international dimension and of opportunities for international careers is broadened. Many such conferences and seminars are open to the community.

HOW ORGANIZED. The Office of International Programs, located in the Graduate School, is primarily responsible for the coordination of international studies. Supporting the director of international programs is a council consisting of persons from each school and from the College of Arts and Sciences. In addition, a corps of international program faculty advise students who are interested in the international studies concentration. Special conferences, seminars, and grant projects are supported through the Office of International Programs in cooperation with the deans of the nine university schools.

For the past five years the university has been affiliated with four other Texas colleges and universities in the Texas Consortium for International Studies. Through this cooperative endeavor faculty and students have conducted research abroad and have participated in a variety of internationally related seminars, symposia, and conferences.

The Office of International Programs is supported by budget allocations from the university. Support also has been received from private and governmental sources for special international programs.

EDUCATIONAL IMPACT. The thrust in international studies has been given a consistently high level of visibility. In the early years this was generated for the most part through special projects such as the Peace Corps Internship Program, the Nigerian Trade Mission, the Houston International Council, and others. Now the emphasis in international studies is being directed toward strengthening the curriculum, enhancing enrichment activities that support faculty development, and encouraging international career opportunities for students. Faculty and student interest in the interdependence of the world community has been heightened. The university's outreach projects offered through the Center for International Development have provided information about trade and finance to the community. This has increased awareness of the university's role as a special institution for urban studies that affect the world community, and vice versa.

RESOURCE PERSON. Joseph Jones, Dean, Graduate School and Director of International Programs, Texas Southern University, Houston, TX 77004. Phone: (713) 527-7232.

U.S. MILITARY ACADEMY, West Point, NY

The U.S. Military Academy (USMA), founded in 1802, has grown from a student body of 10 young men in that year to approximately 4,400 young men and women in 1981. Students represent every state and several countries. The faculty has 545 members, of whom most are active-duty army officers. Approximately 15 percent have tenure. The academy offers a BS degree. Students must complete a 40-course curriculum; 30 are required or core courses. Of the 10 electives, 8 must be concentrated in one of 29 fields. The academy is federally funded.

INTERNATIONAL ASPECTS OF THE CURRICULUM. USMA's core curriculum has nine required courses that help develop an international perspective. During freshman and sophomore years the cadet takes three one-semester courses in a language, of which seven are offered: Arabic, Chinese, French, German, Portuguese, Russian, and Spanish. Also during the freshman year, each cadet takes two one-semester courses in the history of modern Europe or the history of the world or of the United States. During sophomore and junior years, from the Department of Social Sciences, one-semester courses are taken in economics, political science, and international relations. Finally, each cadet takes a one-semester course in military history.

Cadets may pursue the foreign area studies field. One of three areas is selected for concentrated study: the Soviet Union, East Asia, or Latin America. These students must have completed the core language sequence in the appropriate tongue (Russian for the Soviet Union, Chinese for East Asia, Spanish or Portuguese for Latin America). To complete requirements, cadets must take an additional course in the language, as well as electives covering the area's geography, history, and dominant political system(s). Foreign area studies concentrators must take an additional three electives in one of five disciplines: political science, economics, history, geography, or languages. The eighth elective necessary to meet requirements may be selected from an approved list.

In addition to foreign area studies USMA offers several other fields with an international focus, including national security and public affairs (interdisciplinary), economics, geography, international affairs, military history, military studies, modern history, and political science.

Extracurricular activities complement the internationally focused curricular offerings. Among these are sponsorship of the Student Conference on United States Affairs (SCUSA), which has been held annually for 20 years; students representing other colleges and universities participate actively in this curriculum-related, week-long series of plenaries and round tables. SCUSA has attracted national attention and has served as a model for other colleges that have initiated such student conferences. Also, about five cadets participate annually in Operation Crossroads Africa, and there are short-term exchanges with several foreign military academies.

HOW ORGANIZED. Cadets choose their fields of study not earlier than the second semester of their sophomore year. About 30 percent elect internationally focused fields, many because of the relationship between international affairs and their chosen professions.

Committees oversee two of the international fields. The Foreign Area Studies Field Committee, comprising the heads of all departments teaching courses in the field, has responsibility for the organization and development of foreign area studies, while the National Security and Public Affairs Area Committee covers its own interdisciplinary field. Appropriate academic departments are responsible for the other internationally focused fields. No separate funding is provided to any committee or department for such study.

EDUCATIONAL IMPACT. The importance of global study is well accepted at the academy. It is now understood almost universally that United States Armed Forces officers must have an appreciation of the world beyond our borders. The joint operations of World War II and the postwar importance of international alliances for defense are the bedrock upon which this understanding was built. The academy's development of such studies has assisted in influencing the rest of the army toward this more sophisticated view of the world and the role of military power. Officers who have served as academy faculty have been mainly responsible for conveying this view to the army.

RESOURCE PERSON. LTC William R. Calhoun, Jr., Office of the Dean, U.S. Military Academy, West Point, NY 10996. Phone: (914) 938-3122/3881.

U.S. NAVAL ACADEMY, Annapolis, MD

The Naval Academy (USNA) was founded in 1845 at Annapolis and evolved into a four-year undergraduate institution for educating young men and women to be officers in the U.S. Naval Service. It enrolls about 4,500 undergraduates as midshipmen; some 80 percent pursue technical majors in engineering, science, and mathematics, and about 20 percent in the humanities and social sciences. The BS is awarded. There are 550 faculty, with about half civilian academicians (73 percent have doctorates) and the other half officers with advanced degrees from the U.S. Navy, Marine Corps, and other services. A U.S. Foreign Service officer and exchange officers from foreign navies are also on the faculty. The academy is governed by the superintendent (its president), the academic dean, the commandant of midshipmen (dean of students), and senior faculty who comprise the Academic Board, responsible for overall academic decisions. The Academic Advisory Board, comprised of recognized educators and other prominent citizens, advises the administration.

INTERNATIONAL ASPECTS OF THE CURRICULUM. Though international studies were included over the years in core courses in American diplomacy, international law, European history, and seapower, the shift to a system of majors and to a new academic structure placed the responsibility for this primarily in the Political Science Department, which now resides in the Division of United States and International Studies (USIS). Since this division includes the language studies and economics departments, language learning support and complementary courses provide a rigorous international program. The History Department in the humanities division also supports the USIS division curriculum.

Students pursuing international studies generally elect a political science major. In consultation with academic advisors, they design programs in international and comparative politics, including geographic regions. About 10 percent of all midshipmen major in political science, of which almost 60 percent pursue international affairs. Some 70 percent of all other students take one political science elective, with the international courses the most popular.

Language learning had always received high priority at USNA, and only in recent years was the requirement for each midshipman to take two years modified. Midshipmen majoring in political science, economics, English, and history (20 percent of the student body) must complete four semesters of a modern language and may elect further upper-level courses. Students who can validate two college-level years of a language are strongly encouraged to take at least one additional year and to maintain proficiency through various activities such as the language clubs. The Language Studies Department has created a special description for midshipmen on how language studies relate to and enhance their careers and how such study fits into their curriculum.

HOW ORGANIZED. After a general grounding in U.S. politics, international relations, and research methods, midshipmen pursuing international studies concentrate in their areas of interest and take advanced courses in international politics, foreign and national security policies, Communist political systems, and regional studies (Latin America, Asia, Europe, Middle East, and Africa), including research seminars. There are also tutorial independent study opportunities and the Trident Scholar Program, in which students can plumb a given international interest. The recent Trident Scholar Prize was awarded to a history project on U.S. naval policies in China before the establishment of the People's Republic.

Chinese, French, German, Russian, and Spanish are offered at all levels; Japanese may be added. Though there are literature courses, the emphasis is on fluency. Film, slides, magazines, and video cassettes are used. Recorders and cassettes are issued to students for practice combined with regular course homework.

Summer internships are available on a competitive basis: 12 in the Strategic Planning and Politico-Military Affairs divisions of the Department of the Navy; 2 at NATO headquarters in Belgium; and 2 in the Office of the Assistant Secretary of Defense for International Economic Affairs. Over 40 midshipmen are on exchanges with foreign navies each summer for professional training; 8 visit the French and German naval academies. External funds support summer language and area study abroad for about 20 students.

EDUCATIONAL IMPACT. The international dimensions broaden USNA's engineering-oriented curriculum and touch each student. All freshmen study Western civilization since 1715 (with emphases on geography and on social, political, and cultural developments, including the evolution of military institutions and policies) and take a course on seapower (which examines the antecedents and development of the U.S. Naval Service within the framework of the United States' growth as a global power).

In addition, extracurricular activities provide contact with diplomats, academicians, military leaders, journalists, and other international affairs experts. The USIS division sponsors the annual Naval Academy Foreign Affairs Conference (NAFAC), run by midshipmen with faculty advice. Over 200 student delegates prepare position papers for discussion at round tables. The foreign language clubs' meetings, film festivals, formal banquets, and the annual International Ball reach large numbers of midshipmen. The political science, history, and economics clubs organize seminars and forums that bring in distinguished speakers who often address international issues. Also, the History Department holds an annual naval history symposium and has become the nation's principal research and teaching resource in this area.

RESOURCE PERSON. G. P. Atkins, Chairman, Political Science Department, U.S. Naval Academy, Annapolis, MD 21402. Phone: (301) 267-2430.

UNIVERSITY OF MARYLAND BALTIMORE COUNTY
Catonsville, MD

The University of Maryland Baltimore County (UMBC), in the Baltimore suburbs, opened in 1966 and serves some 6,000 undergraduates from the Baltimore-Washington metropolitan area. UMBC offers major programs that lead to the BA in African-American studies, American studies, ancient studies, biological sciences, chemistry, economics, English, geography, history, mathematics, modern languages and linguistics, philosophy, physics, political science, psychology, sociology, theater, and the visual and performing arts. There are also approximately 500 graduate students in biological sciences, chemistry, applied mathematics, policy sciences, psychology, sociology, and education. Faculty number about 300; most have doctorates.

INTERNATIONAL ASPECTS OF THE CURRICULUM. The Department of Modern Languages and Linguistics has developed a new BA program. Instead of separate majors there is one BA in modern languages, with options in one language, two languages, and language and literary studies. Articulation among the options is established by a core of three courses dealing with language, literature, and culture. These courses, taught in English, are taken by all language majors and are accessible to other students as well. They treat the phenomenon of language—its nature, its structures, its social context.

The World of Language. This course, in its third year of operation, begins with the question of the definition of language—visual, auditory, and other sensory and social codes. The course then examines everyday communication, from slang and informal conversation to writing and more formal usage. Language strategies are considered in a variety of cultures.

Textual Analysis. Based on the new and rapidly growing field of semiotics, the course introduces students to theories and techniques of analytical reading and to the interpretation of texts of all kinds—written and pictorial, from the everyday to the poetic. Students learn to approach this material from the points of view of the producer of the text, the receiver, the message, the code, and the context. Projects and workshops are conducted in English for nonmajors, while majors work with French, German, or Spanish texts.

World Language Communities. This course is intended to expand the culture awareness of UMBC students by introducing the study of language in its broad context of historical, political, and social issues. The impact of colonization and linguistic imperialism, the role of religion, and the suppression or extinction of minority languages are discussed. These sociolinguistics problems introduce students to the explosiveness of the language issue in bi- or multilingual states. Finally, the course examines language issues concerning the United States: linguistic and immigration policies, language minorities, the international role of American English in business and science, and other topics.

The department's operational budget is around $12,000. The last two courses were developed under a $50,000 pilot grant from NEH. Moreover, students can earn credits through a January session in Salamanca, Spain; an exchange program with Hannover, Germany; foreign study outreach projects with the inner city; the production of a play in a foreign language; the study of business usage; studies in international film; and an internship program with community groups or appropriate agencies.

HOW ORGANIZED. The curriculum has grown away from the traditional study of national literatures and toward communication skills and intercultural studies. Core courses are team taught by two or three faculty from appropriate fields. Because of high enrollments a lecture format with active student participation is used. In addition, students are involved in workshops, sometimes conducted by other faculty, and small group projects. These courses rely significantly on media and on outside consultants and speakers.

Grades are based on several multiple-choice quizzes, the workshop, and one or more projects. These courses are regularly examined through a departmental evaluation, a university evaluation consisting of a quantitative and a qualitative part, and a report by an outside consultant.

With the exception of two core courses designed with NEH support, courses were developed with departmental resources. These new offerings are being established on a firm basis, as more faculty are trained to teach them and content and scope are continuously improved. Other curriculum development grants are being sought for this purpose.

EDUCATIONAL IMPACT. Because of these innovations in language learning, a number of departments and programs rapidly began recommending to their majors the study of a language. Some emerging patterns hold few surprises: Students in social work, sociology, and nursing are taking Spanish; those in economics, managerial sciences, and music find French and German useful as an elective or part of a double major. The music department, interestingly, seems to exemplify this symbiotic relationship with languages since it has started to offer workshops titled Singing in French or Singing in German. A university committee selected one core course, World of Language, as a requirement for a newly approved BA in photography. The World of Language has continuing enrollments of over 100, up from 50 in its initial offering. The department now has over 60 majors and enrolled over 1,200 students in fall 1980.

RESOURCE PERSON. Claud A. DuVerlie, Project Director, Department of Modern Languages and Linguistics, University of Maryland Baltimore County, Catonsville, MD 21228. Phone: (301) 455-2130.

UNIVERSITY OF MASSACHUSETTS, AMHERST, Amherst, MA

The University of Massachusetts, Amherst (UM/A), located in the Connecticut Valley, is a land-grant institution. Founded in 1863, it joins the neighboring private colleges (Smith, Amherst, Hampshire, and Mount Holyoke) in the Five College Consortium. Enrollment is about 24,000, including 4,000 graduate students. The university consists of the College of Food and Natural Resources, the College of Arts and Sciences, the School of Business Administration, the School of Engineering, the School of Health Sciences, and the School of Physical Education. Some 11,000 students live in dormitories; others live off campus or commute. Faculty number around 1,500. Some 94 majors are offered, plus many special programs and a wide range of extracurricular activities.

INTERNATIONAL ASPECTS OF THE CURRICULUM. International education is multifaceted, including foreign student activities, area studies, overseas study, and faculty exchanges. Over 670 foreign students from 90 countries are enrolled (about two thirds graduate students and one third undergraduates). A range of programs involves foreign students in the international education of the American students and the community, including cross-cultural communication programs, an annual International Fair Week, a host family program, special tutoring in English for foreign student spouses, and many events scheduled by the International Student Association.

Foreign area studies programs include Latin America, the Soviet Union and eastern Europe, Asia, and western Europe. Several programs offer a special certificate. All include films, symposia, visiting lecturers, and special cultural events.

Overseas study programs number close to 40 and include every major world region. UM/A gives special emphasis to student exchanges with higher education institutions abroad for an academic year. These arrangements offer the advantages of in-state tuition for visiting students and guaranteed places at the overseas institutions for UM/A (and Five College) students chosen to participate. Over 300 from UM/A study abroad annually. The newest program is with Beijing Normal University in China; 15 Five College students are studying there.

Through international faculty exchanges a UM/A professor teaches for a semester or academic year at the partner institution while the counterpart teaches at the Amherst campus. They earn each other's salaries. While pay adjustments are sometimes needed to ensure that faculty in either country avoid financial hardship, the exchanges are modest in cost for what they contribute—an international perspective on the disciplines taught and fuller information about other countries and cultures. Because the exchanges tend to continue from year to year, they bring close interinstitutional relationships.

HOW ORGANIZED. The most unusual feature of UM/A's international education program is the student exchange program. This encourages students in the humanities, the sciences, and professional schools to study abroad. For example, an exchange with the University of East Anglia in England will send UM/A chemistry majors there for the junior year while chemistry majors from East Anglia will spend a compulsory year of their degree program at UM/A. These arrangements require careful meshing of the curriculum of the major and close communication between faculty at the two universities. The cost to students, other than travel charges, is little more than if they stayed home, as UM/A students pay "home" fees in the United Kingdom while British students remain eligible for their student grants while in Amherst.

In other UM/A exchanges students go to Nigeria (University of Lagos), Taiwan (Tunghai University), Japan (Sophia University), and elsewhere. Reciprocity is usually through student exchange, but on occasion the partner institution sends a professor to the Amherst campus. For example, under the exchange with Beijing, Chinese faculty come to UM/A for advanced research. Beijing may later send graduate students to UMass (Boston and Amherst).

EDUCATIONAL IMPACT. The international education programs are enthusiastically received at the Amherst campus. Foreign students are among the best enrolled. Students who have been abroad bring back new knowledge (including self-knowledge), new perspectives, and heightened motivation. The faculty exchanges permit UM/A staff to spend time abroad in a period when external funds for overseas travel and research have diminished. The exchanges are especially important in bringing faculty from abroad who inject a different perspective. The international education programs of UM/A have increased so markedly in the last decade that the tone of the campus has become more international. Now many students, rather than thinking study abroad is for someone else, realize that it is a genuine, low-cost opportunity for them.

RESOURCE PERSON. Barbara B. Burn, Director, International Programs, University of Massachusetts, Amherst, MA 01003. Phone: (413) 545-2710.

UNIVERSITY OF MONTEVALLO, Montevallo, AL

The University of Montevallo (UM) is state supported; it has an enrollment of 2,556 and is located in the center of Alabama. Founded in 1896 as a women's institution called Alabama College, it was made coeducational in 1956 and renamed in 1969. The university has four colleges: business, fine arts, education, and arts and sciences.

Maintaining a strong emphasis on the liberal arts as a basis for all curricula, the university has offered an inexpensive, accessible "small college" type of public higher education. The curriculum is based on a broad general education core and includes preparation for business, education, arts and sciences, government, and public service, with undergraduate programs in premed, prelaw, and pre-engineering as well as selected graduate programs. The university has a full-time faculty of 140.

An annual state appropriation funds less than half of the university's annual operating budget. Remaining revenues are generated through sales and services of various auxiliary enterprises, contributions, and tuition.

INTERNATIONAL ASPECTS OF THE CURRICULUM. In its 1978 Mission and Goals Statement the university included a pledge "to give increased attention to promoting international/intercultural programs and activities in the university and the community through a broadly based, coordinated effort," recognizing a decade of development of these areas. The university adopted a broadly based, intercultural, humanistic approach to equip students to function creatively and meaningfully in an increasingly interdependent, global environment. This focus gives priority to activities that lead to greater cultural sensitivity and awareness. The aim has been to add international/intercultural dimensions to all levels of the university through educational experiences that promote interest and involvement and increase the flow of information about other countries. These dimensions have been introduced into academic programs, faculty development, foreign student programs, continuing education, and outreach activities.

The academic core is an interdisciplinary international/intercultural studies (IIS) major/minor which includes, in addition to the general education requirements, course-integrated international study and travel, language study, courses in intercultural communications, and an internship program. Programs are designed individually, often with double majors, combining international/intercultural study with established majors such as business, education, and communications. Internships are arranged in career-related areas within the university and in the community. Also included is an International Summer School, which offers credit for intercultural field experiences provided through independent travel programs or American Institute for Foreign Study (AIFS) programs. Extracurricular activities that enhance the academic programs include a Fulbright Lecture Series, an International Issues Workshop, an International Film Festival, and field trips with international students.

These programs and activities require little institutional funding but use all available resources. Through a cooperative arrangement with AIFS, UM has been able to provide sound travel-study programs with support for faculty from AIFS. This involves no direct institutional funding and enables the university to integrate academic programs and intercultural travel and to provide opportunities for faculty development. Additionally, AIFS has promoted the university credit programs in its announcements, contributing substantially to the development of the International Summer School.

The university participates in the Alabama Consortium for the Development of Higher Education (ACDHE), whose International Programs Committee has a U.S. International Communications Agency grant that provides for faculty travel, an International Issues Seminar, and the Fulbright Lecture Series. Other resources include a National Association for Foreign Student Affairs grant to establish a statewide Foreign Student Association, Danforth grants for a Symposium on Global Education and an international film festival, and an Alabama Council on the Humanities grant for a Festival of Arts program.

HOW ORGANIZED. The director of international/intercultural studies is responsible for coordinating, promoting, and developing international/intercultural programs and activities. The director teaches all IIS courses, advises majors, and administers the International Summer School, reporting to the dean of the College of Arts and Sciences on all academic programs. The director also consults with faculty on all travel programs, working directly with the Office of Continuing Education in developing international/intercultural noncredit programs. The director takes an active part in outreach programs, holding governor's appointments to the Alabama Foreign Trade Relations Commission and as state director of Friendship Force. And the director is responsible for working with faculty and administration to develop proposals for funding, as well as for keeping the university community apprised of international/intercultural developments and opportunities for research and travel.

EDUCATIONAL IMPACT. Faculty and administrators have been involved in international/intercultural activities through participation in a wide variety of programs. The university has been instrumental in initiating and supporting intercultural activities at the national, state, and local levels. In 1978 the president enlisted the cooperation of all Birmingham colleges and universities to support a Friendship Force exchange with Costa Rica. This program involved 508 people and their families in a 19-day cultural exchange. In 1980 some 110 people from Montgomery and Birmingham participated in a Friendship Force exchange with West Berlin.

More than 2,700 people from Alabama, Costa Rica, and West Germany have made personal contacts through Montevallo's programs. A 1981 exchange will involve another 500 families from Alabama with families in Mexico. These activities, in addition to providing intercultural experiences across a broad spectrum of the community, have also created a reservoir of goodwill and support for UM international/intercultural efforts. At least 54 faculty have been directly involved in such activities generated through various travel programs. Intercultural approaches have been proposed for freshman and sophomore English courses and an innovative cultural approach to foreign languages is being offered. The core curriculum committee is considering intercultural requirements.

The university has led in introducing intercultural approaches to international education in the state, offering until recently its only intercultural studies programs. Two ACDHE institutions have received funding to establish centers modeled on the UM center for IIS services.

RESOURCE PERSON. Charlotte Blackmon, Director, International/Intercultural Studies, University of Montevallo, Montevallo, AL 35115. Phone: (205) 665-2521.

UNIVERSITY OF NEBRASKA AT LINCOLN, Lincoln, NE

The University of Nebraska-Lincoln (UN-L), founded in 1869 as a land-grant institution, provides a comprehensive educational program through eight undergraduate colleges, the Graduate College, and the College of Law. Located in the state capital, it is the major university in Nebraska, with colleges of agriculture, architecture, arts and sciences, business administration, engineering and technology, home economics, a Teachers College, and a School of Journalism. Its graduate instruction, the first west of the Mississippi, began in 1886. More than 22,000 from every state and over 100 countries comprise its student body. The university's libraries have some 1,700,000 volumes and 21,000 periodicals. The curriculum offers a variety of interdisciplinary programs as well as the departmental majors and minors in the undergraduate colleges.

INTERNATIONAL ASPECTS OF THE CURRICULUM. In 1976 the faculty of the College of Arts and Sciences approved a new major and minor in international affairs. It offers students an interdisciplinary curriculum that utilizes existing courses. The concept of this international affairs major is limited to relations between nations, including transactions between states (such as diplomacy and war), or between groups within different states (such as corporations engaged in international trade), or between and within international organizations (such as the United Nations), and cultural exchanges between nations. The major and minor were designed to complement the curricula of the existing foreign area study committees. Under the auspices of the Institute for International Studies, a major and minor are offered in Latin-American studies, and minors in Slavic and East European studies and African studies. A minor is also offered by the Asian Studies Committee.

The international affairs curriculum includes courses in the departments of agriculture, agricultural economics, anthropology, economics, geography, history, history and philosophy of education, journalism, management, marketing, political science, and sociology, representing not only the College of Arts and Sciences but Agriculture, Business Administration, Journalism, and the Teachers College. This program attracts a steadily growing number of students. They are encouraged to take advanced language courses beyond the language requirement of the College of Arts and Sciences and to participate in the study-abroad program, which offers opportunities at universities in England, France, Germany, Spain, Mexico, Costa Rica, and Japan for a full academic year.

Through the International Studies Center, under a grant from the U.S. Department of Education, UN-L has enriched its academic offerings in international affairs. The International Scholars-in-Residence program brings prominent scholars in this field from various disciplines and countries for lectures and seminars, and to meet with students and faculty. New international components in existing courses, interdisciplinary courses, and workshops in international affairs enhance the curriculum for students in existing departments as well as in the interdisciplinary programs.

HOW ORGANIZED. The International Affairs Committee, appointed by the dean of the College of Arts and Sciences, supervises the students with majors or minors in international affairs through its coordinator, who also serves as chief advisor. Within the requirements for a major or minor, each student is encouraged to select courses from at least three departments that coincide with his or her area of concentration in international affairs. So that close faculty-student contact may be promoted, every major must include a seminar in international relations or a comparable course of independent study, honors, readings, special problems, or special topics. The International Affairs Committee includes representatives from the faculties of all the departments involved in this interdisciplinary curriculum.

The U.S. Department of Education grant is administered through the International Affairs Center under the direction of the dean and associate dean of the College of Arts and Sciences. Although the International Scholars-in-Residence program and some special workshops and courses depend on this grant, the basic curriculum in international affairs is a permanent part of instruction at UN-L. The International Affairs Committee does not receive or need financial support, as its curriculum is provided by regularly offered courses from the departments.

EDUCATIONAL IMPACT. Faculty and administrators throughout the university have shown exceptional cooperation with the International Affairs Committee and the International Studies Center. A good working relationship exists with the Institute for International Studies and the foreign area study committees. Faculty from various departments and colleges with different interests in international affairs are no longer isolated from each other as they once were. Thus instructors more readily encourage students to enroll in courses offered in different departments. Many more students than those with majors or minors in international affairs have benefited from the programs in international studies.

RESOURCE PERSON. Lloyd E. Ambrosius, Professor, Department of History, University of Nebraska, Lincoln, NE 68588. Phone: (402) 472-3256.

UNIVERSITY OF NORTH CAROLINA AT CHARLOTTE
Charlotte, NC

The University of North Carolina at Charlotte (UNCC) was founded in 1946; in 1965 the North Carolina general assembly made the college a campus of the consolidated University of North Carolina. While primarily an undergraduate institution (over 8,000 full-time students), it also offers master's degrees in 12 disciplines. UNCC has over 9,400 in total, with a full-time faculty of 520 whose average age is under 40 and of whom over 90 percent hold doctorates. With a total physical plant worth $85 million, UNCC's annual budget is over $20 million. UNCC offers 40 degree options in 25 departments. The university is divided into six colleges: architecture, arts and sciences, business administration, engineering, human development and learning, and nursing. Students are primarily from North Carolina (only 300 foreign students and 200 from other states are enrolled), with 80 percent living less than 100 miles away.

INTERNATIONAL ASPECTS OF THE CURRICULUM. Established in 1975, the Center for International Studies is the main coordinating, initiating, and supporting unit for international education on campus. The center was formed to strengthen the international dimension at UNCC, in the community, and in the state; to solidify programs and services for international students; and to support and participate in cooperative programs beyond the university. The center integrates all elements (curriculum, foreign students, study abroad, campus programs, public service programs, consortia, and professional development) into strengthening the international awareness of the campus and the community through the understanding of others.

By offering an undergraduate concentration in international studies the center allows students to pursue an interdisciplinary and comparative study of foreign cultures and societies while they meet requirements for a major in one of the approved university degree programs. In addition to major requirements, students must complete a minimum of eight international courses in at least three other departments and two years of at least one language. The study program to fulfill this option may be viewed from a variety of perspectives: topically, e.g., world population, poverty, violence, and war/peace futures; geographically, e.g., the Soviet Union, Eastern Europe, Africa, Asia, and Latin America; or chronologically, e.g., ancient, medieval, or modern. Most of the 100 students in the program major in business, history, political science, or languages; however, students with any major may earn a concentration in international studies. The concentration draws its offerings from over 150 courses (including interdisciplinary courses) taught by over 60 professors in 12 cooperating departments.

For international students the center provides certification, orientation, individual counseling, liaison with campus and community services related to their needs, academic liaison, immigration assistance, and host family programs.

The center develops study/travel abroad opportunities, with current offerings for undergraduates in the following areas: semester and academic year programs in Copenhagen; fall semester in India; holiday programs to the Caribbean; summer programs in Scandinavia and elsewhere.

HOW ORGANIZED. The Center for International Studies is located within the Division of Research and Public Service; and the director of the center reports to the division's vice chancellor. Professional and support staff of the center consist of the director, three program coordinators, three language instructors, seven secretarial staff, and two part-time student workers. The center receives funds from five sources: state ($60,000), grants ($100,000), contributions ($15,000), contracts ($100,000), and program fees ($290,000).

A variety of events are sponsored by the center for the university and the community. Among these are the annual international festival, International Film Festival Week, the International Club, and international dinners, as well as guest speakers and special programs for international students visiting on exchanges.

Faculty are encouraged to work with the center's staff to arrange exchanges, including the Fulbright program, departmental exchanges, and those based on agreements between UNCC and foreign institutions. The center also funds faculty travel for international study and research, release time for course development or work on a specific international project, and faculty colloquia on international topics.

The center's community activities include symposia on international topics; Great Decisions (Foreign Policy Association)—an annual foreign policy discussion series; international business workshops (programs on aspects of international trade); friendship force (annual community exchange between citizens of Charlotte and those of an international city); community-based programs such as host family, bilingual education, Sister Cities International; and service to individuals and organizations for international information and program development.

EDUCATIONAL IMPACT. The Center for International Studies has had a profound impact on UNCC's development over the past five years. New international courses have been added to the curriculum; interdisciplinary courses have been created, there is increased cooperation from area specialists, language study is encouraged, and faculty receive greater support—all with positive effect on undergraduates. Over 40 faculty are funded annually by the center for research and study; more than 25 programs are sponsored by the center for the university and the community; and travel/study opportunities have increased.

RESOURCE PERSON. Earl L. Backman, Director, University of North Carolina at Charlotte, Center for International Studies, UNCC Station, Charlotte, NC 28223. Phone: (704) 597-2407.

UNIVERSITY OF NORTH CAROLINA AT GREENSBORO
Greensboro, NC

The University of North Carolina at Greensboro (UNC-G) was founded in 1891, became a women's college in 1932, and since 1963 has been a coeducational member of the 16-campus University of North Carolina system. An accredited, state-supported university, UNC-G awards undergraduate, master's, and doctoral degrees, and consists of a College of Arts and Sciences and six professional schools—business and economics; education; health, physical education, and recreation; home economics; music; and nursing. Enrollment is over 10,000. It has an operating budget of $33.5 million and an endowment of $3.3 million. Of the 617 full-time faculty 62 percent hold doctorates.

INTERNATIONAL ASPECTS OF THE CURRICULUM. In the *Self-Instructional Language Program* (SILP) students may study critical languages not available in regular course offerings. For example, though Chinese is spoken by nearly a billion people, it is not yet widely studied in the United States. About 30 students are studying Chinese, Japanese, Hebrew, Arabic, Portuguese, and Hindi through this program. Vietnamese is also available; Swahili and Hausa may soon be added. Many SILP students also participate in the International Studies Program, an interdepartmental plan offering a second major or minor in contemporary global studies.

International departments of various local businesses make use of the Self-Instructional Language Program and students from the Greensboro Regional Consortium for Higher Education (UNC-G plus five other institutions) also enroll. SILP expense is minimal: Total program cost last year was about $3,000.

The program is eight years old and provides two full years of instruction in the languages offered. Standards are rigorous: Only one unexcused absence from a drill session is allowed each semester and a B average must be maintained. Students in the International Studies Program are encouraged to use self-instructional language learning.

HOW ORGANIZED. The program is directed by the UNC-G history professor who started it. He schedules classes, hires and trains native speakers as drill instructors, and screens student applicants. The program includes a student self-evaluation procedure.

Students meet in a weekly one-hour drill session with a native speaker for conversation practice and are expected to study their language at least two hours a day, using tapes and texts. At the end of the semester they are tested by a language professor from an outside institution, taking the same comprehensive examination given to students in regular classes, with sections on speaking, reading, and writing.

SILP credits may be used to satisfy the university's language requirements.

EDUCATIONAL IMPACT. UNC-G students in such diverse disciplines as business and nursing are becoming more aware of global interdependence and opportunities for international employment or travel. Increasingly they seek the additional language studies offered by SILP. Their training has earned them scholarships for study abroad, entry to graduate schools of their choice, and access to careers directly related to the language study.

The success of this program has helped attract external funding for widening international studies on campus. A large part of a three-year global understanding grant from the U.S. Department of Education to the Greensboro Consortium of Colleges and Universities has gone to new language materials, courses, and in-service training for SILP. This permitted creation of branch programs at member institutions.

RESOURCE PERSON. James C. Cooley, Director, Self-Instructional Language Program, University of North Carolina at Greensboro, 315 McIver Street, Greensboro, NC 27412. Phone: (919) 379-5289.

A description of the University of Pennsylvania's approach is presented in The Role of the Scholarly Disciplines, *Change Magazine Press, 1980; E&WV Series I.*

UNIVERSITY OF PITTSBURGH, Pittsburgh, PA

Private, state related, and nonsectarian, the University of Pittsburgh is a complex of 16 schools, 97 departments, 27 special centers, and 4 regional centers serving outlying regions at Greensburg, Johnstown, Bradford, and Titusville. The Pittsburgh campus consists of 52 buildings on 125 acres. Full- and part-time faculty number 2,500 and enrollment is 35,000, of which 23,000 are undergraduates. On the main campus undergraduate enrollment is 18,000, with 8,000 in the College of Arts and Sciences. With the exception of agriculture, the university offers a full range of academic disciplines and professional studies. Emphasis on making the university international began in the early 1960s. The University Center for International Studies was created in 1968 to coordinate these international interests and to promote international dimensions in the various schools and departments.

INTERNATIONAL ASPECTS OF THE CURRICULUM. The *University Center for International Studies* (UCIS) coordinates the teaching, research, public service, and outreach activities. The center's full-time director reports directly to the provost and has a permanent staff of 45. The director's high-level administrative position reflects Pitt's strong commitment to a truly international university. The university provides a budget for center administration and for program development. New programs and expansion of existing programs are usually financed, fully or in part, from external sources. Grants, research projects, and overseas projects involve an average of 40 persons in addition to center staff. Faculty formally associated with the center number 200 and as many more are associated with short-term programs, international contacts, and externally funded projects.

Four of the programs within UCIS—Asian studies, Ethnic studies, Latin-American studies, and Russian and East European studies—offer undergraduate certificates or related concentrations. In these, undergraduates major in a traditional discipline and study in depth a geographic area or a theme. The multidisciplinary approach requires students to supplement their department's courses with at least four related courses in at least two other departments. In addition, students must have two years of college-level language study or its equivalent. In the case of Latin-American studies, a special on-campus seminar followed by a two-month field experience in Latin America is required for the certificate. Majors with a strong international dimension are also available in many traditional departments and courses of study.

UCIS maintains a close relationship with the Study Abroad Office in the College of Arts and Sciences and with the International Student Office. UCIS also houses the Institute for Shipboard Education, a nonprofit organization that contracts with the university for academic sponsorship of the Semester at Sea program, which conducts a curriculum adapted to the world areas covered by a variety of semester-long itineraries. The center sponsors visiting foreign faculty as well as Associates of the American Universities Field Staff who return to member campuses after scholar-reporter tours abroad. Together those groups add an average of 100 persons per year who are available to complement regular faculty and enrich the undergraduate curriculum.

HOW ORGANIZED. The university and the center utilize several strategies to enhance international dimensions. Internal grants are made to professors for curriculum development, research, and travel with an international focus. UCIS organizes and often conducts Freshman Seminars with a focus on world areas and global issues. Schools and departments are encouraged and often helped to revise or add courses that expand area and thematic coverage of the world.

When new faculty are being recruited, UCIS encourages the inclusion of international expertise in criteria for selection. Advice is available for faculty and students for overseas consultancies, fellowships, grants, and exchanges. UCIS provides financial management for funded projects for individuals or groups, or for schools and departments, when asked to do so.

Relationships are maintained with 40 universities and institutes around the world to assure a continuous flow of visitors and bases of operation for university faculty and students. Outreach activities involve faculty and students in community forums and K-12 schools. Timely responses are made to current events in the form of seminars and lectures; and music, art, and drama presentations are made throughout the year.

EDUCATIONAL IMPACT. The university's efforts to emphasize international dimensions have had evident results. Internationalists are found in all schools and departments of the university, with the heaviest concentrations in the faculty of arts and sciences, and the curricula reflect this. A central concern for international studies and global issues education and a centralized unit parallel to the schools provide a valuable service in cutting through content and administrative jurisdictions. UCIS does not own courses or degrees but serves as advocate and facilitator for internationalization throughout the institution. Faculty cooperation across departments takes on an added legitimacy in an international context—interdisciplinarity is understood and endorsed. Faculty and content can be mustered for world area and thematic programs for students.

Undergraduate interest in international studies has not been traditional at the university in spite of great interest at graduate levels and heavy faculty involvement. (The undergraduate student population is less cosmopolitan than the graduate population.) In recent years efforts to move the university's unusually international character into undergraduate levels have had increasing impact and these efforts continue.

About 75 students fulfill requirements for area studies certificates and related concentrations each year. In addition, 5,000 enroll in internationally oriented language, literature, social science, and humanities courses. Other general education courses with a strong international comparative dimension attract 4,000.

RESOURCE PERSON. Burkart Holzner, Director, University Center for International Studies, 4-G Forbes Quadrangle, University of Pittsburgh, Pittsburgh, PA 15260. Phone: (412) 624-1776.

UNIVERSITY OF SOUTH CAROLINA, Columbia, SC

The University of South Carolina (USC) was founded in 1801, the first state college to be supported by annual public appropriations. The nine-campus system (4 four-year and 5 two-year colleges) is the state's oldest and largest public institution. Main campus enrollment is approximately 22,000, with emphasis on the graduate level. Research facilities include a library of over 1.5 million volumes, plus 1.2 million units in microform, and nearly 9,000 current periodicals. An intense building program has resulted in a modern physical plant, including the Physical Sciences Center, Coliseum, College of Nursing, library, Law Center, Biological Sciences Center, College of Business, Physical Education Center, Social Sciences Center, and the James F. Byrnes International Center.

INTERNATIONAL ASPECTS OF THE CURRICULUM. The university has highlighted its commitment to international education through the Department of Government and International Studies, a tenure-track faculty of 45 (the third largest political science faculty in the nation). It offers undergraduate, master's, and doctoral degrees in international studies. In addition, exchange programs with 15 African, Asian, European, and Latin-American nations have been arranged by the colleges of engineering, education, medicine, and business administration. A formal intergovernmental relationship, including universities, has been signed between South Carolina and Shanxi Province, People's Republic of China.

All nondegree international programs and research/service ventures are coordinated under one director in the James F. Byrnes International Center. It houses the North American headquarters of the International Studies Association (which moved its executive offices to the university in 1979), an Earth Sciences and Resources Institute, map depository, educational television studio, the offices of the graduate school, and the Office of Research & Sponsored Programs. The Earth Sciences and Resources Institute has established major grant and contract relationships with Egypt, the United Arab Emirates, Tunisia, Italy, England, and Colombia, and is working on protocols with the People's Republic of China, Yugoslavia, and Nigeria. The College of Business Administration operates the master's in international business program (MIBS), which incorporates internships with many overseas firms. The College of Engineering is the international producer of an engineering-degree-by-media program utilized by many other countries.

The university has a Foreign Dignitaries Program that brings world figures to campus for lectures, seminars, ETV filming, and formal discussions with the South Carolina State Development Board and the office of the governor.

HOW ORGANIZED. The Department of Government and International Studies (in the College of Humanities and Social Sciences) and the College of Business Administration offer internationally focused degrees. The international studies offerings in the department lead to undergraduate majors, an MA, and a doctorate in international studies. In addition, a student may obtain the same degrees in political science with only field specialization in international relations.

Both the government and international studies department and the MIBS program use heavy private and state-appropriated funding. The Institute of International Studies provides graduate research assistance to faculty as well as a variety of research and publication services to faculty and students. Private corporations in South Carolina, which leads the United States in the ratio of foreign direct investment, give extensive assistance to the College of Business Administration.

All degree programs are available to qualified students on the other four-year campuses in the Carolina system. Foreign participation in this program has been facilitated by the fact that one quarter of main campus enrollment is at the graduate level, itself nearly 25 percent international students.

EDUCATIONAL IMPACT. The University and the state have become significantly international in the last five years because of emphasis on a "Window to the World" in the Master Plans I, II, and III for the Carolina system. The state's business community has declared that the higher education system and its international awareness have been instrumental in attracting outside investment, domestic as well as foreign, to South Carolina. The cultural commitment of the state and of USC is exemplified by the annual Spoletto Festival, an international event headquartered in Charleston and displayed throughout the state.

As principal coordinator of all international activities, the James F. Byrnes Center performs official liaison for the state with the Middle East, the Caribbean, Central America, Europe, and the Far East.

RESOURCE PERSON. James A. Kuhlman, Director, James F. Byrnes International Center, University of South Carolina, Columbia, SC 29208. Phone: (803) 777-7810/2933/2675.

UNIVERSITY OF TEXAS, Austin, TX

The University of Texas at Austin is a state institution founded in 1881. Its 46,000 students come from across the nation and from over 100 countries for undergraduate, graduate, and professional education in architecture, business administration, communication, education, engineering, fine arts, law, liberal arts, library science, natural sciences, nursing, pharmacy, public affairs, and social work.

INTERNATIONAL ASPECTS OF THE CURRICULUM. The College of Liberal Arts has seven academic units offering degree programs and concentrations with international content: the Institute of Latin American Studies, the Center for European Studies, the African and Afro-American Studies and Research Center, the Center for Asian Studies, the Center for Mexican American Studies, the Center for Middle Eastern Studies, and the International Studies Program. Enrollment in the undergraduate courses exceeds 7,000; more than 150 students are working toward BAs in these programs and some 125 are earning graduate degrees. In addition, many of the academic departments have study programs of international import and more than 20 languages are regularly taught. An International Programs and Studies Committee fosters and controls a number of exchange programs for undergraduate and graduate students, including arrangements in Europe and South America. Several thousand foreign students are on campus; many are connected to the programs and provide an on-campus exchange. Students can major in a particular area of the world or in the international dimensions of a chosen discipline.

HOW ORGANIZED. The instructional programs are research based and are oriented toward various aspects of civilization and development, especially in the humanistic and social science areas. Each of the area programs is staffed primarily by members of academic departments, some of whom hold part-time appointments in the programs. All programs receive funds from the College of Liberal Arts and many have significant support from federal, private, and international sources. Facilities include the research library of the Latin American Institute. There has been a good deal of collaboration with universities and institutions of other countries.

EDUCATIONAL IMPACT. The international programs have a long tradition at the university. Latin-American studies came first in 1941 and was followed by the others in the 1950s and early 1960s. The goals are to produce well-trained students capable of making significant contributions in academics, business, and national and international service; to create a secure and attractive academic environment in which outstanding scholars can research and teach; and to promote communication and understanding between people of the United States and other countries.

RESOURCE PERSON. John M. Weinstock, Office of the Dean, College of Liberal Arts, University of Texas at Austin, Austin, TX 78712. Phone: (512) 471-4141.

UTICA COLLEGE, Utica, NY

One of Syracuse University's 20 colleges, Utica subscribes to a philosophy of education dedicated to the cultivation of the liberally educated professional. A small coeducational college in a suburban setting, its relationship to Syracuse University offers many advantages usually found only at large institutions, although the college maintains autonomy on matters of curriculum while awarding a Syracuse degree. Over 1,400 full-time and 700 part-time students are enrolled and the faculty has 96 members. An average class size of 20 ensures maximum contact and contributes to a warm student-faculty relationship.

INTERNATIONAL ASPECTS OF THE CURRICULUM. Utica offers a *concentration in International Business* that has brought an international component to three already popular majors—business administration, political science, and international studies. Students with these majors may elect a sequence of courses designed to improve their ability to function in the rapidly growing world of multinational trade and commerce. The concentration consists of courses tailored to eliminate deficits in a student's background that could hamper international performance. For business majors the concentration emphasizes broadening international/intercultural courses in addition to specialized international economics in order to increase sensitivity to the international environment. For political science and international studies majors the concentration focuses on business courses in both introductory and advanced international subjects. The concentration approach has provided considerable flexibility to the program and has enabled international business instruction at Utica to address individual needs while providing solid, realistic preparation for the job market.

Key courses in the international business curriculum consist of World Trade (a basic theory course), Foreign Trade Management (practical fundamentals of export-import documentations, procedures, financing, and operations), International Marketing, Comparative Economic Communities, and Political Economics of the Multinational Corporation. These are complemented by a broad array of intercultural, area studies, and international systems offerings. There is language support in French, Spanish, and German. Other languages may also be offered through the Critical Languages Program, under the auspices of the National Association of Self-Instructional Language Programs. Recent offerings have included Russian, Polish, Hebrew, Arabic, Italian, and Chinese.

The program's development has been closely supervised by an advisory board of international business professionals, who have helped determine the skills, sensitivities, and broad areas of knowledge that are especially in demand among businesses seeking entry-level managers. The business advisory board has been refreshingly consistent in its demand for language training, a sense of business principles, and sensitivity to the diversity of world culture.

HOW ORGANIZED. The international business program is overseen by the director of international programs, a member of the faculty, who is responsible for coordination among the four divisions supporting it. This coordination is essentially limited to avoiding schedule conflicts among key courses and to ensuring consistency in the advising received by students who have an international business focus as part of their majors. The director of international programs is also responsible for keeping in touch with the business advisory board and for convening it when curriculum revision or review seems appropriate.

The developmental costs of the program were borne by a grant from a private benefactor and by a Title VI grant from the U.S. Department of Education. After the development phase (1975-79) the program was fully incorporated into the academic budget of the college, with divisions meeting material and support costs for those courses offered under their auspices. The director of the program is compensated by a reduction in course load.

The program offers an International Business Internship to the best students each summer, providing paid experience in a firm with substantial international activity. These have ranged from multinational banks and manufacturing firms to small exporters.

The diversity of student backgrounds and the different levels of international focus obtained in secondary school led Utica to offer a world survey course to ensure a strong foundation in the current political structure of the state system.

EDUCATIONAL IMPACT. The international business program has created an expanded constituency for the language programs, especially at the intermediate level, and has expanded the international content of several courses. It has opened interdisciplinary lines of communication and has led the college's parent institution to review the program for keys to the effectiveness of this communication. It has shown students in the liberal-arts-focused international studies major that their world affairs interests may lead to a career that is rewarding both personally and financially. Finally, it appears to have led to a growing interest in internationally oriented courses in general; enrollments in these courses are now at a high point. This appears related to general student feelings in these courses that knowledge of the international scene can be applied in various ways.

RESOURCE PERSON. Michael K. Simpson, Utica College of Syracuse University, Burrstone Road, Utica, NY 13502. Phone: (315) 792-3157/3055.

VALDOSTA STATE COLLEGE, Valdosta, GA

Valdosta State College (VSC) originally was chartered in 1906 as a state normal college for women. It opened to students in 1913, offering two years of college work. In 1922 the name was changed to Georgia State Women's College and it became a four-year institution. In the 1930s the college was principally a liberal arts institution and remained so until 1950. At that time Emory University gave its Emory Junior College in Valdosta to the University System Board of Regents, which changed the name to Valdosta State College and made it a coeducational multipurpose senior unit in the university system. The college has a total enrollment of 5,000, with undergraduate work leading to the Associate of Applied Science, the BA in 14 major programs, the BS in 6 major programs, the BS in Education in 9 major programs, the Bachelor of Business Administration in 7 major programs, and the bachelor's degree in nursing, fine arts, and music. There are master's programs in the arts, sciences, and business administration and education specialization. The college has two campuses, a mile apart, that total about 150 acres of a residential section of the south Georgia city of Valdosta.

INTERNATIONAL ASPECTS OF THE CURRICULUM. International studies uses the umbrella approach in sponsorship of international programs. The designation covers three major areas. First, overseas programs use broad cultural approaches in languages, history, culture, speech communication, fine arts, and the entire realm of academic study abroad. Second, the department offers such programs as the Third World Culture Series, which are given for credit to college students and are also available to the public. These have focused on: India, Brazil, Liberia, Nigeria, Japan, and Chinese civilization; the National Model United Nations participation in New York in April and sponsorship on the VSC campus of a Model High School United Nations Assembly; and U.S. State Department programs and appearances by foreign scholars, lecturers, and government officials and diplomats. Third, Valdosta promotes efforts in various departments to increase the international dimension of instruction through area studies, e.g., Asian, Latin-American, Canadian, and European studies, and modern languages.

The conference and programs are financed through a special allocation to the Department of International Studies. Other programs are aided by private contributions and by grants from the U.S. Department of Education, the State Department, and the National Endowment for the Humanities.

HOW ORGANIZED. Since there is no unifying basic curriculum for international studies, the International Education Committee plans, with the administration, in-service sessions for faculty on internationalizing the curriculum in all departments.

The umbrella approach ensures input from all departments and divisions. Representatives of different areas of the college are also included in the International Education Committee and in other collegewide groups.

The college maintains liaison with and representation on a number of important international consortia: the Southern Center for International Studies in Atlanta, the Southern Atlantic States Association for Asian and African Studies, the Georgia Consortium for International Studies, the Southern Consortium for International Education, the American Association for State Colleges and Universities, the Japan-American Society of Georgia, Inc., the China Council of Georgia, the National Collegiate Conference Association (voice for the National Model UN), the National Association for Foreign Student Affairs, and the Southern Conference on Language and Language Teaching.

EDUCATIONAL IMPACT. The overseas programs for public school teachers—such as two Multicultural Understanding Programs in India, in which 55 participated; two Faculty Development Seminars for college teachers in India and Brazil; and the Modern Foreign Language Department programs—have ensured for public schools new courses and new international dimensions to existing courses, plus a heightened awareness of international activities.

RESOURCE PERSON. William M. Gabard, Director of International Studies, Valdosta State College, Valdosta, GA 31601. Phone: (912) 247-3314/3355.

WESTERN KENTUCKY UNIVERSITY, Bowling Green, KY

Founded as a teacher-training institution in 1906 by an act of the Kentucky general assembly, Western Kentucky University consists of seven colleges and offers five baccalaureate, three associate, and eight graduate degrees. There are 51 majors, 62 minors, and 47 areas of concentration, along with a variety of professional and preprofessional curricula. Also offered are 37 2-year associate degree and 3 certificate programs. There are 10,600 undergraduate and 2,800 graduate students enrolled. Western employs 605 full-time and 88 part-time faculty; 59 percent hold doctorates. The annual budget is $42 million; most funding comes from legislative appropriation by the state and the balance from tuition, grants, donations, and other sources.

INTERNATIONAL ASPECTS OF THE CURRICULUM. International education activities at Western include the Latin-American and Asian area studies programs, several study-abroad programs, the faculty and student Fulbright programs, international exchange programs, international projects, and the Office of International Student Affairs. Undergraduate minors in Latin-American and Asian studies are interdisciplinary, drawing courses from art, history, geography, economics, sociology/anthropology, languages, government, religion, and music. The minor requires one year of Spanish or Portuguese or its equivalent, and additional courses in these languages may count toward the minor. Since 1976 a federally funded Center for Latin American Studies at the university has added support to the academic program, built library resources, and provided a community outreach program. Under grant funding, summer stipends have been awarded to faculty on a competitive basis for development of courses relating to Latin America, a beginning course in Portuguese has been funded, and a series of Summer Workshops on Latin America for Teachers has been sponsored.

Western has an overseas program, with summer and winter intersession study available in England, Scotland, and Latin America. There is a full academic year program in France, and student teaching requirements may be met in Guatemala, Costa Rica, Colombia, Belgium, or England. Western's Department of Foreign Languages cooperates with language departments of other Kentucky institutions in offering summer study-abroad programs in France, Austria, and Spain. In addition, special seminars and field research programs are available to Western students, primarily in Latin America. Over the years Western faculty have served as consultants and technical advisors on a variety of projects on Chile, Nicaragua, Venezuela, Guatemala, Nigeria, and other areas. Teacher exchange and the Fulbright programs have brought faculty from institutions abroad to Western's campus and have provided opportunities for Western faculty to teach and do research outside the U.S.

Western has received, in addition to federal funding for the Center for Latin American Studies, three federal grants in the international area. In 1973 there was a two-year Strengthening International Dimensions grant and in summer 1980 a Group Project Abroad for Teachers to study in Guatemala and Costa Rica was funded. Western is now coordinating a federally funded, statewide Citizen Education for Cultural Understanding project. There are 290 international students from 44 countries on campus; they aid the international program as they share their cultures with the university community. About 1,000 students and 60 faculty are involved with international programs at the university.

HOW ORGANIZED. Western's international programs are directed by the assistant vice president for academic affairs, who devotes half time, and are coordinated through an International Education Committee composed of the directors of the respective programs. The directors are faculty; some have reduced course loads to compensate for their administrative tasks. The international academic programs are a core part of the university curriculum; the Center for Latin American Studies, the technical assistance projects, the exchange programs, and the Office of International Student Affairs are permanent and well-supported programs. Funding is included in the university budget, except for the technical assistance projects and the study-abroad programs, which are self-supporting, and for those programs funded by grants.

Western is a charter member of the Kentucky Council for International Education (KCIE), which seeks to promote cooperation in international programs among the institutions of higher education in the state. Its members meet regularly and a newsletter provides information about international activities at the member institutions to the state. Working with the KCIE institutions, Western administers a Kentucky Humanities Council grant which sends "friendship teams" (composed of a faculty advisor, two to four international students, and a student moderator) to Kentucky communities to describe social and cultural life in other countries.

The university's international programs are evaluated individually. An annual evaluation of the Latin American Studies Center by an outside expert on Latin America is required by terms of the grant; study-abroad programs are evaluated by participants and faculty leaders; and a report is submitted annually to the vice president for academic affairs covering all aspects of the university's international education program.

EDUCATIONAL IMPACT. The emphasis on a strong international program is reflected in increased enrollments in language and area studies and by the acceptance of an introductory course on Latin America for general education credit by the university's Academic Council. Seminars and conferences on international topics have been well attended by all segments of the university and have attracted participants from nearby cities as well. Participation in study-abroad and exchange programs continues to increase. A subcommittee on international education has been formed within the university's board of regents. Outside the university a Latin-American lecture series cosponsored by Western and the public library consistently draws well and an annual performance by a Latin-American artist attracts a large community audience. With the university's help the city of Bowling Green reestablished a previous link with Santo Domingo de los Colorados, Ecuador, under the Sister Cities program. Exchange visits have taken place and cooperative projects between the two cities are under way. University faculty are also active in the Kentucky-Ecuador Partners of the Americas.

RESOURCE PERSON. John H. Petersen, Assistant Vice President for Academic Affairs, Office of Academic Affairs, Wetherby Administration Building, Western Kentucky University, Bowling Green, KY 42101. Phone: (502) 745-2298.

WILLIAM PATERSON COLLEGE OF NEW JERSEY, Wayne, NJ

William Paterson College, founded in 1855 as a normal school, has undergone many changes throughout its 125-year history. The most dramatic and comprehensive was its change in the late 1960s to a multipurpose state institution. Situated on a 250-acre hilltop campus, the extensive facility accommodates about 12,000 students, with a full-time faculty of 400. Located 20 miles west of New York City, it is accessible to students from urban, suburban, and rural sections of northern New Jersey. New dormitories will enable the institution to attract students from a wide area. The college offers a variety of undergraduate programs housed in seven schools, along with graduate programs. It is financed by the state and governed by a local nine-member board of trustees.

INTERNATIONAL ASPECTS OF THE CURRICULUM. The interdisciplinary *Honors Program in International Management* is administered through the School of Management. One of five honors programs, it requires that students maintain a 3.0 grade-point average (on a scale of 4.0) while majoring in a discipline such as business, history, sociology, language, etc. The student must complete a multi-disciplinary course that requires command of a foreign language; proficiency in traditional areas such as business, economics, accounting; and a background in sociology, culture, and history of a given region. Three areas of study are offered in the program—Europe, the Far East, and Latin America. Conceptually, the program deals with the fact that the managers of the twenty-first century will have to be multilingual and sensitive to the many cultural forces of the world.

A main task of the language component is to develop cross-cultural units for adaptation in intermediate language classes. Among these are language "seeding" in general cultural notions, business practices and related subtopics such as contracts, and vocabulary terms. Students are encouraged to take the language as early as the freshman year in order to achieve fluency before graduation.

Prominent academic and business speakers are invited to address students in special seminars, as well as in class. Enrollment is limited to 30 to 50.

HOW ORGANIZED. The Honors Program in International Management is managed by a director, usually a business or economics professor from the School of Management who reports directly to the dean. The director coordinates course offerings, advises students, and reviews the curriculum regularly in consultation with the schoolwide curriculum committee. The Honors Program in International Management was initially funded in part from the Foreign Language and Area Studies Title of the National Defense Education Act. Continued support has flowed from the college operating budget and from program improvement funds, separately budgeted by the state for "mission-related programs of high priority."

Internships in both public and private organizations have been arranged for seniors and graduates. To prepare students for this experience and to enhance their marketability after graduation, the curriculum provides a functional knowledge of international economics and business. Periodically the college invites an external program review by experts in international economics and business.

EDUCATIONAL IMPACT. In the past decade academic interest in the international dimensions of management has mushroomed. The American Assembly of Collegiate Schools of Business has mandated the accredited schools of business to incorporate international elements in their curricula. The Honors Program in International Management not only serves as a response to this mandate, but opens the college to a new horizon of multicultural experience. Students have been motivated to learn foreign languages, foreign cultures; indeed, to embrace a whole new learning experience in various disciplines that goes far beyond their national boundaries. The potential and the success of the program are evidenced by the foreign scholarships and internships received by its students. In 1980, for example, three scholarships from Taiwan and a National Science Foundation scholarship were awarded for graduate study. The students also enjoy an advantage in their pursuit of career opportunities because of their internship experience. The college has pledged to support the program's continued operation.

RESOURCE PERSON.   Cho-Kin Leung, Professor, School of Management, William Paterson College of New Jersey, 300 Pompton Road, Wayne, NJ 07470. Phone: (201) 595-2421.

WOODROW WILSON SCHOOL OF PUBLIC AND
INTERNATIONAL AFFAIRS, Princeton, NJ

The Woodrow Wilson School of Princeton University prepares students to lead as public officials or in private life with an active concern for public and international affairs. Founded in the early 1930s as a cooperative enterprise of the departments of economics, history, politics, and sociology, the school reflects the belief that problems of public importance are best approached when their historical roots as well as the interplay of economic, political, and social factors are understood. It is an integral part of Princeton University, a private, coeducational institution founded in 1746 as the College of New Jersey. Princeton has an enrollment of 4,400 undergraduates, a full-time faculty of 620, and a residential 300-acre central campus. Princeton programs emphasize individual responsibility and the free exchange of ideas and opinions. This is reflected in the wide use of preceptorials and seminars, the provision for junior year independent work, and a mandatory senior year thesis.

INTERNATIONAL ASPECTS OF THE CURRICULUM. The Woodrow Wilson School is policy oriented and emphasizes problem solving. It arranges internships and public-sector, curriculum-related jobs, as well as study abroad.

The *Undergraduate Policy Conference in Public Affairs* educates students in the investigation of international and domestic public policy issues. Topics change from year to year and have included Sino-U.S. relations, mass media and communications policy, strategic arms control, federal taxation, U.S. policy in the Middle East, energy policy, and so on. The Undergraduate Policy Conference differs from any course, seminar, or junior year independent work in other departments or schools. By dealing with salient topics for which documentation or readings may be scant, it requires students to seek out public officials and specialists concerned with the conference subject.

After two years of liberal arts preparation sophomores may apply to the school as their junior and senior year major department. Upon admission, students draw up a program of course work for the two years in one of four fields—international affairs, economic problems and policies, government of a democracy, or urban affairs—with identifiable international dimensions. In international affairs, which has been the most popular in recent years, students may concentrate on a region of the world or on the process of modernization and development.

HOW ORGANIZED. The school is an autonomous unit of the university headed by its own dean, who supervises its faculty, budget, and administration. Each student, in designing a program with the assistance of faculty advisors, draws on several academic departments as well as on school programs. Students are strongly encouraged, regardless of specialization, to study philosophy and ethics of public affairs, as well as quantitative techniques such as statistics and computers.

To emphasize the problem-solving approach, the program focuses on clarity in communication, functioning under deadlines, public speaking and debate, group deliberation and decision making. The senior thesis is an in-depth, independent research paper prepared throughout the senior year. The equivalent of two years of language learning is required for graduation; international affairs majors generally go far beyond this. Moreover, those specializing in area studies must reach a higher level of proficiency.

Because of the emphasis on internships, course credit is given for part-time supervised jobs during the academic year in the public sector, support from endowed funds goes to summer field work, and a student's potential to do this phase is evaluated in the admissions process. Study abroad is encouraged and supported in the same manner.

EDUCATIONAL IMPACT. The school provides an interdisciplinary learning experience through the liberal arts and sciences as applied toward professional service in government, law, journalism, diplomacy, education, business, or other sectors. The impact is seen in the demonstrated abilities of graduates to pinpoint the essentials of an issue, to see the larger values at stake, to bring to bear in problem solving several intellectual traditions and approaches, to reach responsible conclusions, to communicate effectively, and to reach accommodation among diverse values as expressed through the group—tasks highly essential in public and international affairs.

RESOURCE PERSON. Michael R. Kagay, Associate Director, Undergraduate Program, Woodrow Wilson School of Public and International Affairs, Princeton University, Princeton, NJ 08544. Phone: (609) 452-4824.

II

Consortia

These descriptions reflect the range of consortial approaches found in the Council on Learning's survey of international programs. Many other effective consortia exist and reach varying numbers of undergraduates. Those presented here have ideas that upon evaluation proved to be highly adaptable or of pertinent interest to other campus efforts for widening international educational dimensions.

COLLEGE CONSORTIUM FOR INTERNATIONAL STUDIES

CCIS was founded in 1972 to provide "international/intercultural learning (abroad) of high quality" for students in the 32 participating colleges and universities in Canada and the United States. The consortium's philosophy is that the undergraduate curriculum should offer an opportunity for all able students to pursue part of their college education overseas. CCIS grew out of the earlier Tri-State Consortium that was made up of pilot colleges in New Jersey, New York, and Pennsylvania. A small grant from a church foundation interested in disseminating the experience of one member, Rockland Community College, led to Tri-State's creation and ultimately to CCIS. The consortium is overseen by officers located at Ocean County College in New Jersey, Rockland in New York, and Harrisburg Area Community College in Pennsylvania.

INTERNATIONAL ASPECTS. During the academic year CCIS offers students from member colleges some 62 overseas academic programs in 25 locations. These semester or yearly programs range from structured, formal courses at affiliated institutions to service-learning and contract/independent study courses. CCIS also sponsors short-term programs of ten days to six weeks during intersession, spring, and summer vacations. The range of programs and courses covers the spectrum of the undergraduate curriculum.

In addition to the principal programs abroad for students, the consortium provides opportunities for professional development of faculty and staff at member institutions. This is accomplished in a number of ways, including parallel study while accompanying students in their academic programs abroad.

HOW ORGANIZED. The presidents of member institutions form the CCIS board of directors, which elects its chairman and oversees the consortium. An executive committee, composed of nine institutional representatives elected by the board to establish policies and guidelines, operates the consortium. The Program Review Committee (subcommittee of the Executive Committee) reviews and evaluates ongoing programs.

Specific programs are sponsored by individual members, who have full responsibility for them and act as their agents throughout the consortium. Although students register for a program on their home campuses, the sponsoring college provides the academic credit involved, keeping transfer payments to a minimum. These tuition payments in most cases cover instructional costs abroad. Students select their courses and structure a full semester program prior to departure. Generally, living and transportation are the only additional costs to the student; these are prepaid and arrangements are handled by the sponsoring consortium member, allowing the student to concentrate fully on the educational program. Students are evaluated prior to admission according to academic ability, maturity, motivation, and potential adaptability to another culture.

CCIS members pay an administrative fee to the sponsoring campus and a pro-rated share of program operating costs based on the number of a member's students sent on a program. Specific policies have been established in the agreements signed by each member. These require student evaluation of the courses and programs.

Since service-learning—fusing experiential learning with that from a mentor—is stressed, the learning contract is an important CCIS facet. A mentor guides formal study and tutorials, advises on the proper mix of independent reading and writing, and supervises the service dimension.

EDUCATIONAL IMPACT. CCIS sends over 1,000 students from member schools abroad annually. This brokering approach to widening international dimensions for undergraduates makes use of an array of educational institutions and environments in the host countries abroad. One fully developed example is Rockland Community College's Israel program, which sends over 200 students each semester to some 38 colleges, universities, agencies, and nonformal settings such as the kibbutz and the development town. As many as 25 sponsoring faculty a year travel with students on such programs. A major attraction to students is the opportunity to study abroad in a service-learning mode.

RESOURCE PERSON. Charles H. Clark, Dean, Harrisburg Area Community College, Harrisburg, PA 17110; phone: (717) 236-9533. William Lavundi, Ocean County College, Toms River, NJ 08753; phone: (201) 255-4000. Gerhard Hess, Director of International Education, Rockland Centre for International Studies, Rockland Community College, Suffern, NY 10901; phone: (914) 356-0160.

COMMUNITY COLLEGES FOR INTERNATIONAL DEVELOPMENT

CCID, also known as The Cooperative, was formed in 1976 and now consists of nine community and junior college members: five on the East Coast, two in the Midwest, and two on the West Coast. The Cooperative was created to widen international dimensions in the curriculum and to promote world understanding through educational links with like institutions in other countries. The stated CCID mission in this area is "to identify, develop, and expand mutually beneficial relationships which contribute to the improvement of college programs, services, and staff." Much of the mission is accomplished by providing for the professional enrichment of faculty, staff, and students and by sharing resources and expertise with other countries having similar concerns in occupational, vocational, and technical education.

INTERNATIONAL ASPECTS. The Cooperative provides most directly for members' international curricula through overseas centers that supervise structured study-abroad programs for members' students. The other major direct curricular activity is an annual international education conference held by CCID for program directors, staff, faculty, presidents, and trustees. The purpose of this conference is to guide curriculum planning and staff development, with participants returning to their institutions to implement instructional evaluation and design and to conduct faculty renewal programs.

The most significant work of The Cooperative is seen in its creation of bilateral framework agreements between CCID and education agencies in other countries. Although each agreement is designed according to the needs and strengths of the signatories, it generally accomplishes its objectives through faculty and resource exchanges. A Suriname Agreement (1979) provides for training 133 Surinamese teachers in the United States over a three-year period in technical areas deemed essential by Suriname. CCID colleges involved will draw on these visitors to enrich the cultural aspects of their curricula. An agreement with Taiwan (1980) is designed to improve technical education in Taiwan's professional colleges and integrate Chinese culture into U.S. two-year colleges. This will be achieved through the exchange of presidents, other administrators, and faculty; in-service training of Taiwanese faculty in the United States and Taiwan; delivery of educational materials to the colleges involved; and other development activities.

HOW ORGANIZED. The Cooperative operates with a minimum of administrative overhead. Each member undertakes coordination of specific tasks or programs. For example, a 1980 symposium for two-year college presidents from around the country was conducted by the Seattle Community College District; its 1981 international education conference was coordinated by the Waukesha County Technical Institute; obtaining the Taiwan agreement was organized by Brevard Community College.

The Cooperative is governed by a board of directors consisting of the presidents of its members. The board's administrative arm is an executive director, currently situated at Brevard. CCID has dues, receives in-kind contributions from its members, and has obtained external funding for its operational programs. Bilateral agreements often seek to minimize costs by having each party identify and use its particular strengths. For example, Taiwan's Education Ministry might pay all faculty exchange transportation whereas the host American college would pay all compensation differentials for both Chinese and Americans involved. The aim is to use financial resources efficiently and avoid bureaucratic constraints.

EDUCATIONAL IMPACT. This approach may be most significant for generating top-level commitment to an international curriculum. It has been important enough to attract external support, especially from the U.S. Department of Education, for making the curriculum international, for providing foreign curriculum consultants, and for Group Study Abroad awards. Because of the benefits derived from The Cooperative's first international forum on postsecondary midlevel manpower training, it also received funding from the Organization of American States and the Tinker Foundation.

American technological advances have led to increased demand for CCID services by developing countries' technical education agencies. Formal training programs have been established for other governments or U.S. organizations and other technical assistance has been provided. In addition, CCID facilitates these countries' study of the community and junior college concept for meeting development needs. Some 20 countries have taken advantage of this and in turn have had the potential of reaching almost 300,000 individual students at Cooperative colleges.

RESOURCE PERSON. Robert Breuder, Executive Director, c/o Brevard Community College, 1519 Clearlake Road, Cocoa, FL 32922. Phone: (305) 636-6621.

CONSORTIUM FOR INTERNATIONAL STUDIES EDUCATION

CISE is an institutional subscriber organization of 45 colleges and universities that seek to improve the quality of international studies education in the curriculum. Established in 1972 as a postsecondary network for developing, testing, and disseminating innovative materials, CISE is affiliated with the International Studies Association (ISA) as its educational service arm. It evolved from the former ISA Education Commission that was designed to cover the entire spectrum from K-12 through continuing education. Subsequently undergraduate education became the focus.

INTERNATIONAL ASPECTS. The consortium concentrates on getting knowledge in international studies into the classroom. It promotes the production and use of materials and courses or modules which reflect international and global issues knowledge and have demonstrated instructional validity. CISE also provides a continuous forum for reviewing educational objectives, materials, and methodologies in international studies.

CISE makes instructors, usually in the humanities and social sciences, aware of the importance of international studies and assists the generalist who must teach in a wide variety of specialized areas. It bridges the gap between, on the one hand, scholars doing research on international subjects and the knowledge they produce and, on the other, those teaching undergraduates and in need of suitable materials. An underlying philosophy is that most faculty must become thoroughly familiar with international materials, most of which are not in traditional textbook form, before they can or will adopt these for classroom use.

CISE differs from many other programmatic organizations, such as the Foreign Policy Association, which provides educational materials like the Great Decisions program. It recognizes the importance and legitimacy of those teaching international dimensions. Rather than simply providing monographs and pamphlets, CISE involves faculty in developing, testing, and using internationally oriented modules and courses.

HOW ORGANIZED. The consortium is governed by an executive committee elected from institutional representatives, which in turn chooses the CISE chairman. The only administrative staff are the executive director and a part-time secretary. The executive director comes from the faculty of a member institution. Coordination is accomplished by telephone conference calls. Costs are covered by dues; the bulk is applied to a member's faculty participation in the summer workshop. Programs and development of curricular modules often receive external funding—from the U.S. Department of Education, the National Science Foundation, and the Exxon Education Foundation, for example. This usually is on a one-time basis to accomplish a specific task.

CISE fulfills its goals primarily through the summer workshop, which combines in intensive seminars people who prepare international edcational materials with those who would use the materials in class. The executive committee works with a small group of specialists and members' representatives to plan, coordinate, and conduct each year's workshop, held in a residential situation on a member campus. The recent one at Franklin and Marshall College focused on three areas: global issues, with newly developed student handbooks for eight issues viewed from four perspectives; national security, with the aid of that program at New

York University and in cooperation with the National Strategy Information Center; and international affairs in a broad sense.

Because commercial publishing houses eschew production of particular types of educational materials, CISE performs its own editing and publishing functions. The grants received are used for these purposes after materials are developed. Proposed materials are evaluated in the summer workshops.

EDUCATIONAL IMPACT. Over 700 teaching faculty have taken summer workshops and over 30,000 course modules or sets of other educational materials have been disseminated since CISE was created, mostly through college bookstores. Almost two thirds of summer workshop participants come from non-member institutions. Because CISE materials are offered at 10 to 20 percent of the cost of typical textbooks, classroom use has been greatly enhanced.

RESOURCE PERSON. B. Thomas Trout, Chairman, CISE, Department of Political Science, University of New Hampshire, Durham, NH 03824; phone: (603) 862-1752. James E. Harf, Executive Director, CISE, Department of Political Science, The Ohio State University, Derby Hall 223, Columbus, OH 43210; phone: (614) 422-8130.

GREAT LAKES COLLEGES ASSOCIATION

GLCA is an academic consortium of 12 independent liberal arts colleges. Its collaborative activities include the development and maintenance of off-campus programs that provide students special academic, experiential, and intercultural opportunities. GLCA encompasses a collective student population of over 20,000 and some 1,500 faculty. The association was formed in 1961 primarily with international studies in mind; member colleges were afraid they would be unable to support independently their individual international programs and sought cooperative ways to draw on each other's strengths. GLCA founders, however, had the vision to provide other needed services and programs, including faculty development activities, a women's studies program, and a small colleges office in Washington, D.C., to look after GLCA interests. In addition to its overseas studies programs, GLCA offers a New York arts program, a Philadelphia urban semester, the Newberry Library Program in the Humanities, and the Oak Ridge Science Semester. The association's highest priority has been to strengthen member colleges' academic programs.

INTERNATIONAL ASPECTS.   Through agent colleges or in cooperation with the Associated Colleges of the Midwest (ACM), 13 other liberal arts colleges, GLCA offers eight programs abroad: in Japan, Latin America, Scotland, Africa, European comparative urban studies, Chinese studies, Yugoslavia, and in India. The joint GLCA/ACM program in Japan is the oldest and has provided a model on which others could be built.* It has created a broad base for Japanese studies through Earlham College, which pioneered curriculum, faculty, and student program development in this region. One student program provides preservice training in a Japanese public school. The major Japan program is a cooperative student and faculty exchange between GLCA and Waseda University in Tokyo. Each participating student must complete a special orientation program at Earlham before going to Japan, where the summer beginning the program is spent with a Japanese farm family prior to matriculation at Waseda.

The African programs (administered by Kalamazoo College) focus on the anglophone countries of Ghana, Kenya, Liberia, Nigeria, and Sierra Leone, and on francophone Senegal. The Chinese studies programs are in Taiwan (administered by Oberlin) and Hong Kong with a follow-on Taiwan option (administered by ACM). The European urban studies series visits Great Britain, The Netherlands, and Yugoslavia (administered by Antioch). GLCA faculty (or ACM for joint programs) accompany students as resident directors on each of these.

GLCA also conducts faculty development workshops and conferences with international or country themes. These ultimately provide for course enrichment and the diffusion of salient international dimensions throughout the curriculum. The 1980 conference emphasized the inclusion of Latin-American materials in regularly taught courses in a number of disciplines and the sharing of information about resources and methods appropriate to teaching at GLCA colleges.

HOW ORGANIZED.   The association is governed by a board of directors comprised of the member colleges' presidents, a chief academic officer selected by GLCA colleagues, and three faculty elected by the member colleges on a rotating basis. The board is advised by the academic council, made up of two faculty from each member college plus the three on the board. The deans' council includes the chief academic officers of each college and is charged with overseeing the academic quality of each program. A series of advisory committees draws on faculty and administration expertise from each member college to serve the various programs. All of this is tied together by a president, a vice president, and a small staff at the central GLCA headquarters in Ann Arbor.·

Students at GLCA colleges consult with their campus representatives prior to applying for any program. Other eligible students apply directly to the program concerned. Once a program is chosen, the agent college handles the student's administrative details. Financial aid granted by a home campus usually continues for students enrolled in GLCA programs. The agent college issues the academic credit for the sponsored program; this credit is assured within the association. Program fees take into account the average costs at member colleges.

EDUCATIONAL IMPACT.   Nationally recognized scholars external to GLCA have said that the association has actively and effectively spread interest in and comprehension of other cultures and societies throughout the Midwest. The widening of international dimensions in courses and teaching methods, personal and professional enhancement, and greater public understanding derived through members' outreach programs (ranging from art exhibits to business seminars) have been widely reported. Faculty who begin GLCA seminars report that these lead them into other GLCA activities.

RESOURCE PERSON.   Jon W. Fuller, President, or Donn Neal, Vice President, Great Lakes Colleges Association, Suite 240, 220 Collingwood, Ann Arbor, MI 40103. Phone: (313) 761-4833.

For details see chapter on Earlham College, Richmond, IN, in The Role of the Scholarly Disciplines, *Change Magazine Press, 1980; E&WV Series I.*

INTERNATIONAL/INTERCULTURAL CONSORTIUM

IIC consists of 50 community and junior colleges committed to pooling resources and facilitating interinstitutional access to the international expertise of members. Established by the American Association of Community and Junior Colleges (AACJC) in 1976 upon recommendation by a number of colleges, the consortium grew out of a need to respond to the question of interdependence and its meaning to the member institutions and their communities. Many founding members were already engaged in curriculum development, study abroad, and international exchanges; they recognized the need to share resources and make these more widely available throughout the two-year college community. IIC is primarily a service organization that works through its members to reach consortium goals.

INTERNATIONAL ASPECTS. The consortium emphasizes a symbiotic "Global Agenda"—bringing the world to the campus and the campus into the world. The former is being accomplished by widening international dimensions in the curriculum, through extracurricular activities, and by integration of international students and faculty at member colleges. The latter is being achieved through study abroad, off-campus programs, technical assistance to other countries, and international exchanges.

IIC provides an information clearinghouse and newsletter on international opportunities and programs at home and abroad, on student study/travel/work abroad programs, and on funding availabilities in various international and intercultural areas. IIC gives immediate access to over 50 study-abroad programs offered by its members. Its secretariat provides liaison to federal offices dealing with international affairs and subjects, and to other educational associations involved in international programs. The consortium also assists member colleges in establishing working relationships with institutions in other countries interested in exchange of faculty, students, or educational material. The consortium aids members in cooperative development of model programs on campus and overseas. And IIC sponsors and organizes conferences and workshops to help colleagues share ideas and work on international and intercultural programs.

A major cooperative approach taken by the consortium has been the "lead college" concept, whereby a designated member college applies for funding on behalf of IIC as well as for itself. In 1980, for example, Johnson County Community College developed and obtained a U.S. Department of Education grant to establish resources for international studies training; part of this is an IIC component. This concept has been broadened to include citizen education for cultural understanding and group projects abroad.

The consortium has also created a roster of international education consultants from the IIC membership. They will provide expertise to other members on an at-cost basis for actual expenses.

HOW ORGANIZED. The Executive Committee, comprised of 12 college presidents elected from the membership, oversees the consortium. Programs are generally effected through a number of committees. The Advisory Committee works on issues of special concern and timeliness; its current effort deals with international student services. The Global Assistance in Technical Education Committee handles requests from outside the consortium. The Faculty/Student Exchange/Study Programs Committee works on proposed exchange plans. The

Curriculum Committee is most actively concerned with reflecting the world in the classroom, as well as with planning the annual IIC conference held in conjunction with the yearly AACJC meeting.

Generally the institutional representative is the chief executive officer of the member college. The AACJC director of international services serves as the IIC staff director and provides the secretariat for the consortium as established by AACJC. Funding is provided from an annual fee. Other funding comes from grants developed by member colleges under the lead college concept for specific common interest tasks and programs, such as studies and surveys. The monthly newsletter is the principal means of information dissemination among the members. Other special publications are issued from time to time, such as the annual listing of study-abroad opportunities available from member institutions.

EDUCATIONAL IMPACT. A significant result of the consortium has been enhancement of international dimensions on member campuses through idea sharing by colleagues. Its publication and dissemination activities have helped create a critical leadership in the two-year college community, where international studies have become a growth sector. The IIC approach has helped members avoid the trial-and-error method of providing increasingly needed campus programs and services in the international/intercultural area. The consortium covers some 25 states, and 500,000 students in institutions whose enrollments vary from 800 to 135,000. The consortium's approach and effectiveness have increased membership and widened interest among two-year colleges.

RESOURCE PERSON. Director of International Services, American Association of Community and Junior Colleges, Suite 410, One Dupont Circle, N.W., Washington, DC 20036. Phone: (202) 293-7050.

PACIFIC NORTHWEST INTERNATIONAL/INTERCULTURAL EDUCATION CONSORTIUM

PNIIEC was established in 1979 to promote effectively the diffusion of international dimensions in the curriculum and to foster cultural interaction and intercultural activities. Some 31 academic and nonacademic institutions located in Alaska, Oregon, Washington, and British Columbia comprise its membership. These include two- and four-year, public and private colleges and universities, as well as cultural and community world affairs organizations. The aims are to assist one another in bringing global perspectives into members' curricula, in expanding members' overseas programs, in improving international student services, and in nurturing international awareness in the surrounding communities. A significant impetus in the creation of the consortium was budgetary constraints that precluded development of new international or intercultural activities. The immediate consortium objective is resource sharing and cooperative use of funding. As an umbrella organization, the consortium's different parts appeal to different members.

INTERNATIONAL ASPECTS. The first set of interinstitutional agreements provided for member college students to participate in other members' study-abroad or international cooperative education programs. This allows the student's home institution to award the credit earned and thus retain credit fees (which vary widely among members).

Another arrangement provides for faculty and program development seminars. By means of a half dozen consortium-sponsored conferences over the first year, interinstitutional cooperation was greatly enhanced in addition to the in-service education received on a variety of international topics. These seminars are the core of the faculty activities, with special emphasis on curriculum development. One major part of this is a series of workshops whereby faculty develop individual modules on various issues that can be immediately used in courses being taught or planned. The detailed two-year schedule for this will cover 243 faculty.

By drawing on the strengths of schools and organizations that have established international programs, those without are able to integrate their curricula without high start-up costs. The key factor is flexibility so that each member can develop or expand the programs and services as needed. One major program is the Pacific Lutheran University agreement with Fort Steilacoom Community College, under PNIIEC aegis, to coordinate their international studies programs. This enables Fort Steilacoom students to transfer directly to PLU and pursue foreign area studies without interrupting or prolonging their baccalaureate progress. Such pairing of nearby member schools is an effective method stressed by the consortium.

The purpose of these programs is to help faculty bring international perspectives into the classroom, whether by helping set up international studies degree programs or by implementing faculty training and renewal. The emphasis is thus on citizen education for global understanding rather than on training scholars and specialized professionals in international affairs.

HOW ORGANIZED. A board of directors composed of representatives from each member institution determines consortium policy. An executive committee chosen from among institutional representatives oversees the consortium.

PNIIEC stresses that the institutional representative should be someone active in the curriculum, and not simply a highly placed administrator, so that the member institution gets the most benefit from its participation. The chair of the consortium is chosen from among the executive committee. A small staff consisting of a coordinator, training coordinator, and program assistant serves the consortium; additional part-time assistance is brought in as needed.

The consortium is funded by annual dues and external funding is sought for major outreach and curriculum development programs, especially those focusing on faculty renewal. The consortium serves as a common applicant for funding so that members do not compete for scarce international education moneys.

The consortium serves also as a clearinghouse on international education activities. It distributes information about members' study-abroad and travel programs; in this it provides some quality control by endorsing selected study trips. Although each campus controls its own students' orientation and academic work on study trips, the consortium shares among its members the orientation materials and instructional resources for these trips.

The major training approach chosen by PNIIEC is a three-level set of workshops. First is the development workshop in which designated faculty experts from certain member institutions design educational workshop plans that cover a number of topics and areas and can be implemented by various members. These are then evaluated and tested in planning workshops attended by potential users. The final stage is a series of implementation workshops with faculty at the member institutions.

EDUCATIONAL IMPACT. The major result of PNIIEC has been the creation of a highly effective regional network in foreign language and international studies that has permitted a good degree of rationalization of resources. At the same time, it has generated greatly renewed activity in international and intercultural learning. Its initial success and promise won for it a major U. S. Department of Education grant for citizen education for global understanding. This grant provides even for reaching out through local media to educate on international and intercultural affairs; PNIIEC has received radio and television programming commitments for this.

The convergence of two earlier efforts in Washington and Oregon that resulted in PNIIEC reflects not only greater national interest in global perspectives in education but also the increasing importance of international trade in the Pacific Northwest economy. The academic goal may have priority but the wider perspective is kept in mind. Although an unusual mix, the consortium is perceived by many Pacific Northwest leaders as a means of widening international understanding throughout the region.

RESOURCE PERSON. Mordechai Rozanski, Chair, PNIIEC, c/o Pacific Lutheran University, Tacoma, WA 98447; phone: (206) 383-7628. Michael Gordon, Coordinator, PNIIEC, Northwest Program Development and Coordination Center, 1701 Broadway, Seattle, WA 98122; phone: (206) 587-5423.

III

More Good Ideas

Many excellent ideas for widening international education were found in the survey of programs, not all of which could receive detailed descriptions. More information about the following may be had by contacting the institutions directly. Addresses and telephone numbers are found in such standard references as the National Center for Education Statistics Education Directory, Colleges & Universities, Peterson's Annual Guide to Undergraduate Study, Peterson's/Lippincott Higher Education Exchange: Directory, Marketplace, Almanac.

MORE GOOD IDEAS. . .

In the Council on Learning's national survey of interesting and workable international education programs, numerous worthwhile ideas emerged that could not be listed under the descriptions in Parts I and II of this handbook. Here are just some of the many imaginative approaches that do not attempt to reinvent the wheel.

Many colleges and universities are now choosing to create coherent programs or majors in international studies. These are often interdisciplinary in nature; most tend to be coordinated either by one department (history or political science) or by a center. **Baldwin-Wallace College** (Berea, OH) has an interdisciplinary international studies major coordinated by an international studies committee whose faculty director receives release time for this purpose. **Manhattan College** (The Bronx, NY) has created both international studies and peace studies programs, each coordinated by a committee headed by a faculty director. The former takes a traditional topic and area approach and requires six advanced language credits. The latter looks at peace and social justice and requires 12 language credits.

    SUNY College at Brockport (Brockport, NY) has developed a global studies major/minor. This builds on a multidisciplinary approach of existing course offerings to which have been added special course designs focusing on global perspectives. The program contains skill requirements in quantitative analysis, research, and problem solving. **Towson State University** (Towson, MD) offers an interdisciplinary international studies major as well as thematic area study options in Latin-American, Asian, and African-American studies, and uses a coordinator plus a faculty committee for supervision. The **University of California, Davis** (Davis, CA) offers an international relations major that covers the traditional disciplinary diversity of the field. Its interdepartmental committee reports to the associate dean of the College of Letters and Science. The Davis program includes a substantial foreign language learning requirement. As a major research university with a substantial undergraduate enrollment, the **University of Minnesota** (Minneapolis, MN) offers a number of strong programs that are coordinated through its Harold Scott Quigley Center of International Studies, which is a part of the new Hubert H. Humphrey Institute of Public Affairs. One major undergraduate program offers a minor in foreign studies that is a cross-college, interdisciplinary, individualized program requiring 10 weeks of study abroad and proficiency in the appropriate language, which could include 15 credits of language study.

    Both language studies and area studies programs are offered at many colleges and universities. **Dartmouth College** (Hanover, NH) offers one of the most effective approaches to language learning in the country. Pioneered by Professor John Rassias, his approach has been adopted at more than 38 other schools. Dartmouth's language enrollments have grown substantially over the last decade. **Tulane University** (New Orleans, LA), in addition to its Latin-American and Asian studies programs, recently reinstituted a language requirement for graduation. The decision received wide faculty, student, and administration suppport. **Arizona State University** (Tempe, AZ) has centers for Asian and Latin-American studies which coordinate interdisciplinary undergraduate options or minors. There is also a special program integrating foreign language studies from the College of Liberal Arts with specialized offerings of its Business College. **Florida International University** (Miami, FL) has a Latin-American and Caribbean Center that offers an interdisciplinary area studies certificate to traditional undergraduates and to continuing education students. **Pennslvania State University** (University Park, PA) carries on a number of strong area studies majors and options, most administered by interdepartmental committees. Study abroad is encouraged and

149

this is overseen by the Office of Foreign Studies under the Vice President for Undergraduate Studies. Penn State is also pushing in new directions in language learning, with courses in Russian technical translation and business French.

San Diego State University (San Diego, CA) offers majors and/or minors in a number of area studies, including Asian, African, Afro-American, European, Latin-American, Middle East, Russian and East European, and Chicano studies. The **University of California, San Diego** (La Jolla, CA), in addition to more traditional international studies, has a Mexican studies center with undergraduate offerings. The **University of Pennsylvania** (Philadelphia, PA) has organized international and area studies at the undergraduate level within the departmental humanities and social science curricula as well as through interdisciplinary program committees. The international relations major requires advanced course work in other languages and cultures. The **University of Wisconsin-Madison** (Madison, WI) Dean of International Studies and Programs oversees a number of area studies and topical programs; among the more notable is its African Studies Program. **Vanderbilt University** (Nashville, TN) offers area studies in Latin-American, East Asian, and Slavic areas, which build on course offerings in regular departments. Vanderbilt has a language admissions requirement and requires undergraduates to take courses in six of seven areas, one of which is language studies.

Colleges and universities that have worked at integrating their curricula to provide for diffusion of international and intercultural dimensions throughout campus life are far fewer in number. The reasons for this are many, and often relate to the difficulty encountered in building a campus-wide commitment to this approach. **Earlham College** (Richmond, IN) is considered a pioneer in this regard and reviewed its offerings in the late 1950s to cast the college more internationally. The result was a panoply of language and international programs that have served as models around the country. The Japanese studies program became its strength with more students taking courses dealing exclusively with Japan and its culture than any other American liberal arts college (nine other institutions have larger Japanese studies enrollments, but they are large universities with enrollments over 20,000). Earlham has also taken a novel approach and created "super," "accelerated," and "intensive" language learning options.

North Park College (Chicago, IL) has followed up its commitment to diffuse international dimensions by creating special strengths in international affairs, language studies, and area studies, as well as in college-supported extracurriclar activities that draw on outside associations with international concerns. One example is that all political science courses are taught comparatively; the initial course is not American government but introduction to politics. Another is the commitment to language learning with a two-year requirement for graduation that stresses building on a student's pior language learning. North Park was one of a few colleges that runs successful annual international festivals.

Trinity College (Hartford, CT) has traditionally offered a quality liberal arts education in which international dimensions receive serious attention. Nearly every course listing encompasses international or intercultural topics. Language study is required and language tables, a Spanish club, and a French section in one dormitory have been created. Trinity is also known for its intercultural studies program which offers an established major; its director reports to the dean of the faculty. An international relations major is coordinated by a loose interdepartmental committee.

Antioch International, a separate division of **Antioch University** (Yellow Springs, OH), runs a special series of degree programs around the world. It creates study situations in various locations and accepts transient students from other colleges and universities. About 400 students are abroad in Antioch international programs in any academic year. The dean of Antioch International is assisted by an advisory committee at Yellow Springs. **Bergen Community College** (Paramus, NJ) has created an impressive roster of experts lecturing on various international topics. It has done this through its Center for Public Media Programming which prepares TV courses broadcast by CBS stations around the United States. Called Sunrise Semester, this is a combined seminar and TV lecture course featuring videotapes of internationally known figures like Theodore White, Arthur Schlesinger, Jr., and A. Doak Barnett of The Brookings Institution. As part of the larger set of TV course offerings for students unable to get to classrooms, this international course ultimately reaches about one million viewers beyond the 50 or so registered Bergen students.

Bunker Hill Community College (Charlestown, MA), surrounded by a bastion of prestigious four-year institutions with strong language and international programs, has been able to develop its own internationally oriented curriculum through faculty development seminars. One resourceful professor initiated this process, obtained minimal funding, negotiated necessary release time, and has developed a dynamic set of workshops that attracts widespread faculty interest for the creation of course modules on international subjects. **The College of Staten Island** of the City University of New York (Staten Island, NY) developed the Center for International Service which offers a four-year program combining liberal arts career courses relating to the Foreign Service, international organizations, multinational business, public health, engineering science, and education. In a region where borough colleges were not perceived to be centers of global learning, this program built on existing offerings and added a minimum of new courses, tying together studies in the humanities, social sciences, and professional areas in innovative ways. **Indiana University** (Bloomington, IN) is nationally known for a number of international and area studies strengths. It recently created a Center for Global Studies, which is charged with the responsibility for promoting undergraduate international studies instruction on all Indiana University campuses. The center has a network of faculty representatives from the main and branch campuses. They monitor developments elsewhere and initiate curriculum review and faculty workshops at their respective institutions. Other projects are undertaken by the center itself. The **University of Denver** (Denver, CO) founded the Center for Teaching International Relations in 1968 (located in the Graduate School of International Studies). In addition to its graduate program, the center focuses on in-service teacher education and global studies curriculum development and dissemination. Although primarily aimed at teachers in primary and secondary schools, the center's programs are highly adaptable and pertinent to undergraduate teaching.

Among the special purpose institutions surveyed and others with alternative approaches to infusing international dimensions were a few particularly noteworthy for their strong commitment and innovations. The School of International Service in the College of Public and International Affairs at **American University** (Washington, DC) is the focal point for a wide range of curriculum-related activities in international affairs. Pan Ethnon, one of the larger international relations clubs found (with a membership of over 150), acts as an informal seminar featuring major international speakers. It sponsors an annual International Week that rivals some of the top student foreign affairs conferences elsewhere. In addition, there are numerous language clubs, a Model UN club, a strong foreign student association, and an international dormitory of the caliber of the nation's International Houses. The School of International Service (SIS) and the College of Public and International Affairs also offer strong language and area studies programs which focus on proficiency and multidisciplinary understanding. SIS recently created an innovative bachelor of arts in European Integration.

Albright College (Reading, PA) also is experimenting with widening international dimensions through extracurricular activities. Its International Week/International Day programs have focused on international issues. Albright has widened the content of its international studies through study abroad and through a Washington Semester done in conjunction with American University. Although the **American Graduate School of International Management** (Glendale, AZ) curriculum is at a higher and professional level, many of its ideas and approaches are directly applicable to undergraduate business education as well. **Brigham Young University** (Provo, UT), because of its preparatory work for Latter Day Saints student special missions abroad, features a series of intensive language programs integrated with that professional preparation. **Columbia University** (New York, NY) School of International Affairs has established an accelerated program that brings college seniors into the masters program while completing their undergraduate requirements. This dovetailing of curricula avoids duplication and reduces tuition costs for the student. It also gives students access to innovative language programs such as French Conversation for Administrators and Diplomats (coordinated through the Institute of Western Europe). Columbia is also known for its undergraduate Contemporary Civilizations core in the Columbia College curriculum. **Davis & Elkins College** (Elkins, WV) has created a sophomore level general education requirement in World Cultures, developed with seed money from the U. S. Department of Education. This was established by the humanities division which took the view that a small college in a big world had a significant role of providing fundamental student understanding of key elements of global interdependence.

    Friends World College (Huntington, NY) has focused entirely on "world education" and has designed a curriculum of campus orientation studies integrated with field experience around the globe. This requires two years of study abroad in two cultures other than the student's own. Each graduate in effect completes a double major, one in a traditional discipline and the second in "world education." **The Monterey Institute of International Studies** (Monterey, CA) focuses on international learning for professional purposes. Its intensive foreign language courses integrate learning about cultural, social, political, and economic aspects of the culture involved. **Schiller College** (Heidelberg, Federal Republic of Germany; U.S. office: Arlington, VA) is a multicampus system based in Europe with instruction in English. Because of the cultural and travel programs integrated into its curriculum, it provides a total multicultural learning experience. The **United States Air Force Academy** (Colorado Springs, CO), within its traditional approach to language and international studies, has taken an innovative direction in its humanities curriculum. All cadets must take *Europe and the World since 1500*, organized around the principle of treating all civilizations on equal terms, thus imparting a world view. It places the student in the most familiar civilization first, then moves outward to the others. The **University of Oregon** (Eugene, OR) recently created a bachelor's degree in international studies which requires courses in three cluster areas—international relations, regional cultures/area studies, and global perspectives and issues. It also requires advanced foreign language proficiency.

    Numerous consortial and interinstitutional arrangements are being widely used. Many colleges and universities find this one of the most effective ways to bring international dimensions into the curriculum. The **Consortium on Peace Research, Education, and Development** (COPRED, Bethel College, North Newton, KS) is a campus-based organization that takes the peace-studies approach to international education. It provides classroom materials, an information clearinghouse, newsletters and journal; runs conferences, seminars, and workshops for faculty; and coordinates an action network in this area. The **Kentucky Council for International Education**(KCIE, Western Kentucky University, Bowling Green, KY) is a state-wide consortium whose principal activities are study-abroad and faculty group-projects-abroad programs. KCIE also advances international education through cooperation with the state councils on the humanities and on social studies. The **Ohio College Association** (Capital University, Columbus, OH) recently embarked on an international program of curricular development, international student services, study abroad and experiential learning opportunities, and cultural, athletic, and artistic exchanges.

    The **Pennsylvania Council for International Education** (PaCIE, Beaver College, PA) is a state-wide consortium of higher education and volunteer/civic organizations engaged in international education and exchanges. Its decade-long efforts have been to foster long-term growth of international education within Pennsylvania, develop interinstitutional cooperation and communication, conduct joint projects abroad, and promote state agency support of international education. This group comes closest to the purposes and ideas of the state commissions suggested in the report of the President's Commission on Foreign Language and International Studies. The **Southern California Conference on International Studies** (SCCOIS, UCLA, Los Angeles, CA) is a comprehensive curriculum-oriented consortium of public and private four-year institutions. It has arranged extensive cross-registration for language courses, conducts joint seminars on timely international affairs topics, monitors international education programs, disseminates information on international resources in the region, and runs joint educational programs overseas among its many activities. Over its first eight years it has widened student access to international expertise and learning; in the Los Angeles area, for example, a student is offered some 80 language courses. SCCOIS has allowed member institutions to focus on their strengths and draw on shared resources where they are weaker. Like many consortia, it does not have a paid staff but uses the resources of its members. Its effectiveness stems from emphasizing contiguous Southern California resources.

The **University of Connecticut/Connecticut State Colleges** Undergraduate International Studies Program (UC/CSC International Studies Program, University of Connecticut, Storrs, CT) was recently established to serve primarily freshmen and sophomores on member campuses. It is concerned with curriculum development and improvement of instruction, fosters cooperation with community and technical colleges to enrich international studies, and promotes the development and sharing of resources. It introduced a series of team-taught courses in global and area studies, created a Mobile Outreach Team, and conducted a series of state-wide conferences and workshops for members' faculty and administrators. The **University of North Carolina at Chapel Hill** (Chapel Hill, NC) and **Duke University** (Durham, NC) have entered into an agreement for cross-registration in any courses offered. Because of different strengths each has in foreign language and international studies, this bilateral arrangement has widened opportunities for undergraduates in that metropolitan area.

A final note on consortia—national educational associations around One Dupont Circle in Washington, DC recently established an umbrella organization in international education. The **Consortium for International Cooperation in Higher Education** (CICHE, Washington, DC) has access to over 2,000 campuses through membership affiliation and overseas affiliations with over 50 countries. Although its purposes are outwardly oriented, it benefits the undergraduate experience by bringing into American institutions a greater number of international faculty and by studying problems of mutual concern in international education.

A number of the colleges and universities evaluated draw on the resources of outside organizations that provide class materials or particular programs that deepen the international experiences of their students. Most of these are thematic in character or cover particular regions of the world. The **American Universities Field Staff** (Hanover, NH) offers a wide range of international services that contribute to students' global understanding. It provides international internships in different parts of the world for field research at the undergraduate level. AUFS also conducts a summer seminar on different global topics each year for American and international students in a residential format at its Institute of World Affairs in Salisbury, CT. One significant professional program is its *Workshop for Journalists on Third World Development*; some 20 journalism majors are among the 30 participants at each of these sessions.

The **Foreign Policy Association** (New York, NY) offers a wide range of materials and conducts numerous forums for the public at large. One special educational program is a quarter-century old—*Great Decisions*. Although over 250 colleges and universities use the Great Decisions course, only a few of those surveyed reported this. This annual study/discussion program can be used in a variety of formats and is organized around the Great Decisions book which provides background on eight key issues in U.S. foreign policy. These vary from year to year. Some colleges offer this for credit, others as modules within regular courses. This flexible and adaptable approach provides balanced content for classroom use and features references to films and filmstrips keyed to the eight topics.

The **Institute for World Order** (New York, NY) has developed the World Order studies curriculum model that has been adopted by a number of institutions. This is especially suited for liberal arts curricula. The Transnational Academic Program updates the curriculum guide from time to time. The **Institute of International Education** (New York, NY) widely recognized for its whole range of educational services, recently established a lecture bureau for visiting foreign scholars. Created to encourage the wider sharing of the rich intellectual, cultural, and scientific resources brought to the United States by international visitors, this computerized, up-to-date service is available to any institution. **InterFuture** (New York, NY) is a voluntary organization that provides select college students with the opportunity to carry out academically rigorous, individually planned study projects on important issues in industrialized and developing countries around the world. Financed mostly through contributions, IF provides partial or full scholarships to the selected students.

The **National Strategy Information Center** (New York, NY and Washington, DC) has for two decades provided classroom materials used widely by colleges and universities; it conducts educational programs in international security affairs. The **Scandinavian Seminar** (New York, NY), among its many activities relating to Nordic countries, conducts year-long study abroad programs for undergraduates. Some 150 colleges and universities give academic credit for these programs. The **Society for Intercultural Education, Training and Research** (SIETAR, Georgetown University, Washington, DC) is an educational group concerned with intercultural communication. Its publications and workshops help faculty develop syllabi and modules for classroom use. The **United Nations Association of the United States of America** (UNA-USA, New York, NY) and its local chapters and divisions provide a range of educational services used by many institutions. It recently started an education project aimed at enhancing instruction about the UN and global issues in curricula at all levels. It also provides special background materials for Model UN's and general class use.

These ideas and programs reflect the many different but often parallel approaches taken to provide or enhance international dimensions in the undergraduate curriculum. These are obviously not the only noteworthy programs, but are representative of the pluralism in American higher education. The selections were chosen from among the evaluated institutions and consortia as well as from materials gathered on outside support organizations.

IV

Thematic Index

Colleges and universities cited in this national assessment have been indexed under general program theme or pedagogic approach categories. Some listings may be found in more than one thematic section. Placement under a particular heading is based upon the description of the institution's programs as provided in this volume.

INTEGRATED CURRICULUM

Institutions listed here have made serious efforts in the diffusion and integration of global perspectives throughout their undergraduate curricula.

Brevard Community College, *8*

Donnelly College, *20*

Eastern Kentucky University, *24*

Eisenhower College of Rochester Institute of Technology, *28*

Emory University, *30*

Georgetown University School of Foreign Service, *32*

Johnson County Community College, *42*

Lewis and Clark College, *50*

Monroe Community College, *62*

Mt. Hood Community College, *64*

Pacific Lutheran University, *72*

Reed College, *78*

Rockland Community College, *80*

St. Anselm's College, *82*

School for International Training, *88*

University of Pittsburgh, *116*

Valdosta State College, *124*

Woodrow Wilson School of Public and International Affairs, Princeton University, *130*

STUDY ABROAD

Listings under this heading include a wide range of study-abroad and student exchange programs, faculty exchanges, and programs for specialized international experiences.

California State University and Colleges, *10*

Dickinson College, *18*

Drew University, *22*

Eckerd College, *26*

Georgetown University School of Foreign Service, *32*

Goshen College, *34*

Kalamazoo College, *44*

Lewis and Clark College, *50*

Lock Haven State College, *52*

Middlebury College, *58*

Occidental College, *66*

Pomona College, *74*

Rockland Community College, *80*

St. Olaf College, *86*

Spelman College, *90*

Stanford University, *92*

State University of New York at Albany, *94*

United States Naval Academy, *102*

University of Massachusetts, Amherst, *106*

Western Kentucky University, *126*

Woodrow Wilson School of Public and International Affairs, Princeton University, *130*

CROSS-CULTURAL AND INTERDISCIPLINARY

A wide range of area studies, international relations, cross- and interdisciplinary offerings, and combined major-minor programs are included under this listing.

Central College of Iowa, *12*

Central Virginia Community College, *14*

Colgate University, *16*

Dickinson College, *18*

Eckerd College, *26*

Goshen College, *34*

Goucher College, *36*

Hampton Institute *38*

Hood College, *40*
Lafayette College, *46*
Lehigh University, *48*
Lock Haven State College, *52*
Macalester College, *54*
Michigan State University, *56*
Middlesex County College, *60*
Mt. Hood Community College, *64*
Occidental College, *66*
Ohio State University, *68*
Ohio University, *70*
Pacific Lutheran University, *72*
Pomona College, *74*
Ramapo College of New Jersey, *76*
Rockland Community College, *80*
St. Edward's University, *84*
School for International Training, *88*
Texas Southern University, *98*

United States Military Academy, *100*
United States Naval Academy, *102*
University of Massachusetts, Amherst, *106*
University of Montevallo, *108*
University of Nebraska at Lincoln, *110*
University of North Carolina at Charlotte, *112*
University of Pittsburgh, *116*
University of South Carolina, *118*
University of Texas at Austin, *120*
Utica College, *122*
Western Kentucky University, *126*
William Paterson College of New Jersey, *128*
Woodrow Wilson School of Public and International Affairs, Princeton University, *130*

FOREIGN LANGUAGES

Listed here are institutions evidencing especially strong and imaginative approaches to language instruction and to combinations of language with related fields.

Central Virginia Community College, *14*
Donnelly College, *20*
Georgetown University School of Foreign Service, *32*
Hampton Institute, *38*
Hood College, *40*
Middlebury College, *58*
Ohio State University, *68*
Ohio University, *70*
Pomona College, *74*
St. Anselm's College, *82*

School for International Training, *88*
Stanford University, *92*
State University of New York at Albany, *94*
Tarrant County Junior College, *96*
United States Military Academy, *100*
United States Naval Academy, *102*
University of Maryland Baltimore County, *104*
University of North Carolina at Greensboro, *114*

SPECIALIZED INSTITUTIONS

Listed below is a group of special-purpose institutions with notable strengths and professional approaches in international programs.

Eisenhower College of Rochester Institute of Technology, *28*
Georgetown University School of Foreign Service, *32*
School for International Training, *88*

United States Military Academy, *100*
United States Naval Academy, *102*
Woodrow Wilson School of Public and International Affairs, Princeton University, *130*

1981 Publications in the Education and the World View Series

The Role of the Scholarly Disciplines

This book focuses on the potential role of the disciplines in encouraging enlarged international dimensions in the undergraduate curriculum; it also provides useful insights into campus initiatives and effective curricular approaches.   **$4.95**

The World in the Curriculum: Curricular Strategies for the 21st Century

Written by Humphrey Tonkin of the University of Pennsylvania, this volume considers concrete, feasible recommendations for strengthening the international perspective of the undergraduate curriculum at academic institutions; it provides a guide to meaningful curricular change for top administrators and faculty.   **$6.95**

Education for a Global Century: Issues and Some Solutions

A reference handbook for faculty and administrators who wish to start or strengthen language and international programs, this contains descriptions of exemplary programs, definitions of minimal competencies in students' international awareness and knowledge, and recommendations of the project's national task force.   **$7.95**

Education and the World View

A book edition of Change's special issue on Education and the World View for use by trustees, faculty, and administrators; it also contains proceedings of a national conference that considered the implications of educational ethnocentrism and action to encourage change.   **$6.95**

What College Students Know About Their World

An important new national assessment of American freshmen and seniors, conducted by the Educational Testing Service, that covers the strengths and weaknesses of American college students' global understanding; an aid to faculty and program directors, it pinpoints areas for improving international content.   **$5.95**

ETS National Survey of Global Understanding

The full report of the 1980 national assessment of 3,000 college students about world cultures, foreign languages, and contemporary world issues. With complete data, charts, and analysis.   **$10.95**

NOTES

NOTES

NOTES

NOTES

NOTES

NOTES

NOTES

NOTES